CAROLINA
Beach Music
COMPILATION ALBUMS

CAROLINA
Beach Music
COMPILATION ALBUMS

· THE CLASSICS ·

RICK SIMMONS

THE
History
PRESS

Published by The History Press
Charleston, SC
www.historypress.com

Copyright © 2025 by James R. Simmons
All rights reserved

First published 2025

Manufactured in the United States

ISBN 9781467157728

Library of Congress Control Number: 2024947406

CONTENTS

PREFACE

I've done four books about music prior to this, and three—*Carolina Beach Music: The Classic Years* (The History Press, 2011), *Carolina Beach Music from the '60s to the '80s: The New Wave* (The History Press, 2013) and *The Carolina Beach Music Encyclopedia* (McFarland, 2018)—are, as the titles indicate, about beach music. The strange thing is, every time I do one, I swear it will be the last one. Yet here I am again, writing a book about beach music. The truth is, despite the fact that I generally confine myself to beach music that you could have listened to on a 45 or album prior to 1980, there's always something new to say and something new to write about.

During my two-decade-plus career as a college professor, I primarily wrote about literature, but when it came to writing for pleasure, I seemed to have an affinity for two things: regional South Carolina history and Carolina beach music. That's why, eight books in, four (inclusive) of my books have been about Carolina beach music.

However, loving something isn't enough to justify a book about it, but filling a void in our collective knowledge about a subject is. But you may be wondering why this book, why a book about beach music compilation albums? I think this book fills a need and feeds a market eager to read about classic beach music, and while a few books have come out about beach music, this is the first solely about beach music compilation albums.

What jump-started this book was a comment on Facebook. Though I'm not a big Facebook user, I still have pages for my two History Press beach music books that were published a decade ago. Occasionally I'll publish a picture of an old beach music concert poster or album cover with a few comments for nostalgic purposes, and in May 2023, I posted a picture of an old beach music album along with some information about it. Chris Jones replied with something along the lines of "I'd love to see a book about the beach music albums." That got me thinking—why not? I'd done a lot of research on the albums while working on other things, so much so that I'd planned an appendix on albums in two earlier books but removed them due to space limitations. I'd even interviewed many people instrumental in the creation of the albums. People were obviously interested, so why not? And the idea to do this book was just that simple.

The execution, however, was not quite so simple. Despite the fact that I knew what I wanted to do and had a pretty good idea of how to do it, I realized once I had signed my contract to do this book I had accumulated way too much material. Mark Twain once wrote, "I didn't have time to write a short letter, so I wrote a long one instead," and this applies to books as well. Being concise and knowing what to leave in and what to take out is not always easy. My proposal said I intended to do a book that would look at the first fifteen years of beach music compilation albums, from 1967 through 1981–82, beginning with Atlantic Records' *Beach Beat* in 1967 and continuing up through albums by Bell Records, Arista, Ripete and Warner Brothers. By the time I was well into writing the book, I'd come close to hitting my maximum word count in just the chapters on the first seven compilation albums that came out by 1980 and hadn't even addressed the eight that came out in 1981 and 1982. It was pretty clear that in this book there was no way to do an extensive evaluation of those later albums, so in chapter 7 I simply talk about them briefly as what was yet to come. More than that will perhaps have to wait for another book.

In the meantime, I hope you enjoy this one and hope it contributes to filling the void that exists when it comes to knowing all there is to know about one of the greatest of southern traditions, Carolina beach music.

ACKNOWLEDGEMENTS

A book—and especially a book like this—can be nothing without the help and insight of a number of people. Of the featured artists and performers I talked to whose music appears in this book, I wish to thank Gary Barker and John Barker of the Catalinas, Archie Bell, Norm Burnett of the Tymes, Joe Clinard of Cannonball, Clifford Curry, Carl Gardner of the Coasters, Ken Houston of the Band of Oz, Ken Knox of the Chairmen of the Board, Bob Kuban, Meadowlark Lemon of the Globetrotters, John McElrath of the Swingin' Medallions, Bobby Moore Jr. of Bobby Moore and the Rhythm Aces, Deacon John Moore, Wayne Pittman of the O'Kaysions, Charles Pope of the Tams, Dianne Pope, Jeff Reid of the Fantastic Shakers, Billy Scott of the Georgia Prophets, Bobbie Smith of the Spinners, Ammon Tharp of Bill Deal and Rhondels, Donny Trexler of Bob Collins and the Fabulous Five, Sonny Turner of the Platters and Brenton Wood. Unfortunately, since the songs on these albums are by older artists as a rule, the ensuing decade has seen quite a few of them pass away since I interviewed them.

For background on the albums, I'd like to thank Marion Carter, Deane Morris and the late Ed Weiss (Charlie Brown), and for inspiration and suggestions and other general help I'd like to thank Chris Beachley, Chris Jones, Paige Sawyer, Woody Lynch and Ricky Saucier. I'd also like to thank my student editors: Bristol Cannon, Morgan Edwards, Gabby Geathers, Evan Player, Emily Pilot and Isaac Sanchez Ruffino. Finally, to my wonderful family: to Sue, my wife and copy editor at home, as well as Courtenay, Cord, Matt, Mackenzie, Sutton and Nina. Without your love and support, there'd be no book. My heartfelt thanks.

INTRODUCTION

A Little Background on Carolina Beach Music and Beach Music Compilation Albums

First to address the elephant that is always in the room, that being the question, "What is Carolina beach music?" I'm going to assume that if you're reading this book, and especially if you purchased it, you know what beach music is. Consequently, I'm not going to spend a lot of time defining it, but I will note that something new I have is an article that Chris Jones sent me, a music review by Joel Selvin. Selvin wrote,

> *Beach music has nothing to do with surf music. For more than 20 years, these sounds have provided the soundtrack to summer vacations for three generations of Southern teens flocking to beach resorts like Myrtle Beach, South Carolina, where swimming, sunning, drinking, and dancing to rhythm and blues records are the order of the day....But it is not just regulation rhythm and blues hits that these kids dance the shag to; these are obscure records, some reaching national popularity, but most relegated to regional obscurity. Some are old and some are new. The frothy beat is the thing.*

I think Selvin does a good job of explaining beach music, especially since he was writing in the *San Francisco Examiner* in 1982 in his review for the *Ocean Drive* albums that I cover in chapters 5 and 7. I think his definition is basically what beach music still should be, but over the years, that seems to have changed. Up until the early 1980s, it wasn't all that difficult to determine what was and what was not beach music. After that—and you see the first signs of this on some of the last albums I cover in this book—the somewhat dichotomous relationship between what was beach music and shag music developed (for those of you who may not know, the "shag" is the official dance of beach music). They are not the same thing, and just because you can shag to a song, it doesn't necessarily mean it is beach music. I'm not sure that differentiation even existed until the 1980s, but over the years, as that core of several hundred solid beach songs was anthologized again and again, DJs as well as record producers started looking for ways to broaden the beach music—really, the shag music—spectrum. If you look at so-called beach music playlists today, you see a mix of music and basically none of it is what you find on the albums in this book.

As for the beach music compilation albums, before 1967's *Beach Beat*, they simply didn't exist. In today's world, you go to Apple Music, put the song title in the search bar and voilà!—there it is. There are a lot of options, of course—you can buy a song as a single digital file or as part of a collection. But it wasn't always this easy, and in fact, if a record was an "oldie," it could be downright impossible to find one to purchase. As someone who started collecting beach music 45s in the late 1970s, it was tough even then. And frankly, other than a few places such as Myrtle Beach's Beach Music Center or the Wax Museum in Charlotte (neither of which exist today), it was hard to find old records in the Carolinas. 45s were great of course, but what if you wanted multiple songs for a party and didn't want to play them one at a time or didn't have a DJ?

These are some of the problems that led to the first beach music compilation album, Atlantic Records' *Beach Beat* in 1967. A few albums came out after that, almost in a trickle, but it wasn't until 1980 that the market really opened up. The first Warner's *Ocean Drive* album came out that year, as did the first Ripete album, *Beach Music Classics*. Suddenly, acquiring beach music became a whole lot simpler.

Those albums came out at just the right time for me too. Growing up in South Carolina, I spent a lot of time at the beach, and during my high school years I got really interested in beach music. I fell in love with it even more when I entered Clemson University and joined Kappa Alpha Order, because many of the bands we booked for fraternity parties, like the Catalinas, Georgia Prophets and Embers (to name a few) were also considered beach music bands. I hadn't been old enough to purchase the Atlantic albums or the Bell album when they came out, but I purchased most of the rest of the albums in this book in college or right after. For people who loved beach music, it's hard to describe how eventful it was to suddenly be able to purchase these collections of classics.

Not long after these collections finally became available on LPs, things started to change with the introduction of the first compact disc in 1982. Albums had outlived the popularity of the unreliable 8-track tape, but according to *Retro Manufacturing*, by 1988 CD sales had surpassed vinyl LPs. That made things for collectors easier still, but within a few years, beach music compilations on vinyl were basically a thing of the past.

Like many things in the past, the passage of time makes us look at them fondly, and at the same time, it makes our memories hazy and the acquisition of knowledge about those things harder to find. This book, then, is about those beach music compilation albums produced in the early classic years of beach music, before CDs and before there started to be a delineation between beach music and shag music. I hope it will provide you with some fond memories and give you information about a few things you didn't know about before.

A Note on a Few Final Details and a Guide to Reading the Write-Ups

In the first seven chapters, I examine an album in each chapter in chronological order by the year the album was released. After an introduction with commentary by an individual who was instrumental in the production and sale of the album, I look at the songs on the album in the order they appear on the album, noting the track listings exactly as they appear on the album. Sometimes the album covers had misspellings or slightly mistitled songs or even variation in group names, and I usually point this out.

After each song, I list the year the song was originally released, and in the text that follows, I talk about any pertinent information, including the songwriters, performers and even how the record fared on the charts. Since almost every song discussion lists chart positions, rather than cite the same source in every paragraph, let me note that all chart information comes from the four *Billboard* chart books by Joel Whitburn found in the works cited section. When possible, I also include the performers' own thoughts about the songs. There are few performer insights on the albums in chapters

1 through 3, mainly because by the time I started interviewing the artists around 2010, many of them who had recorded the older songs on Atlantic, King, Chess, Federal and others had passed away. There are more interviews and insights as I examine the later albums, however, and by 1980's *Beach Beat Classics*, I have interviews with seven of the eight artists who have songs on side one and three of the eight older songs on side two.

Sometimes I refer to a song as a "second-level" or "second-tier" beach song, and this is not meant to be an insult. It simply means that a song isn't as well established as songs that have been considered beach songs longer or perhaps that are more popular in beach music circles. For example, while the Georgia Prophets' "California" and "I Got the Fever are undoubtedly first-tier beach classics, their "Nobody Loves Me Like You Do" or "Don't You Think It's Time" are second level. They are great songs but not quite as well established or as beloved as "California" and "I Got the Fever." Almost every classic beach music artist has these, and it would be ludicrous to say the Showmen's "In Paradise" is as beloved as "39-21-40 Shape," or that the Swingin' Medallions "She Drives Me Out of My Mind" is as well-regarded as "Double Shot."

Also, some of these albums have a few odd songs on them, usually songs the record company owned the rights to but that aren't really beach music, and they were used as filler. In these cases, and with songs such as "G.T.O.," "Little Girl" and a few others, there is only a brief write-up of a couple of sentences. They decidedly are *not* beach music, so I really saw no reason to get into a lot of background on them. In the case of songs that are solid R&B songs by beach music artists but are not generally considered beach music anymore (such as "I, Who Have Nothing" or "Without Love (There Is Nothing)"), they basically get the full treatment because when they were put on the albums they were often considered beach music, even if their popularity did not endure.

Finally, if there are multiple songs by the same artist on an album, I often tell part of the artists' story or biography under one song and continue it on another, especially if some parts are more relevant to one song than another. On later albums, rather than rewriting the same biographical information, I write something such as "For background on the Drifters' early years see the entry for 'Money Honey' in chapter 1 on *Beach Beat.*" When later albums include a repeated song from an earlier entry, I don't repeat the entry but instead write something such as, "This is a repeated track from Atlantic's *Beach Beat Vol. 2.* See that album for details about the song."

1

THE FIRST BEACH MUSIC COMPILATION ALBUM: *BEACH BEAT*

ATLANTIC RECORDS 8140, 1967

*I*n order to understand the origin of the first beach music compilation albums, it's important to know about the late Ed Weiss, known as Charlie Brown to beach music aficionados everywhere. He got into the DJ business early and went by "Charlie Brown" (after the popular Coasters song) at the suggestion of a radio station where he worked. After

he graduated from UNC, he eventually worked at WKIX in Raleigh, where he became one of the "KIX Men of Music," DJs extraordinaire. Over the years, he had a number of accomplishments, and at the time of his passing in 2022 he was still doing his weekly *On the Beach* show.

In this case, the reader has to know about Ed Weiss in order to understand the origin of those first beach music albums, and you need look no further than the back cover of the first two *Beach Beat* albums to see his name. Fortunately, Ed was someone I corresponded with a number of times, talked to on the phone several other times and interviewed for my first three beach music books. He was always gracious and willing to share a good story, and he had plenty of them. There was no one better to talk to about the *Beach Beat* albums—because they were basically his idea.

"The story is that Jerry Wexler wanted to do a beach music album, but actually Jerry didn't even know what beach music was," Weiss said. "He was a friend of mine, but what happened was that for years a lot of that music on Atlantic wasn't available—you couldn't get it. When I started working in Raleigh in 1964, a friend's family owned the Record Bar music stores which had originated in North Carolina. They were getting calls for a lot of those [old Atlantic songs], and then I started playing them at night. Songs like 'Nip Sip' and 'One Mint Julep.'" Weiss continued,

> *I figured what the hell, and so I went ahead and called Jerry Wexler at Atlantic Records—this probably would have been in '65. Well, Jerry Wexler had hired a guy named Jerry Greenberg to be his right-hand man. His job was to follow through on things Jerry didn't have time to do because Jerry was a producer—one of the world's greatest. So, Jerry Greenberg and I were talking and I said, "Look—can't we do this damn album? You've got all this music there, we got people down here who want to buy, we got a distributor down here who says he can sell it—is there some way we can make this thing happen?" And we did. So, between having a distributor and a retailer and someone who had time to listen, we put the album out.*

Atlantic as a sponsoring label certainly made sense, because the label had one of the finest catalogues of R&B anywhere. Atlantic and its subsidiary label Atco had artists such as the Clovers and Drifters who were established beach music royalty even then, and newer (in the mid-'60s, at least) artists such as Barbara Lewis and Willie Tee were turning out multiple hits loved by beach music listeners. Even artists with just one strong beach song, such as Doris Troy and "Stick" McGhee, or a group such as the Coasters, known more for novelty records than beach music, were all in the Atlantic or Atco stable of artists.

When the album finally came together, perhaps what seemed most curious were some of the choices that were made, and anyone looking at the track listing today would probably have a few questions. For example, why use Drifters songs such as "Money Honey" and "Honey Love" instead

of "Under the Boardwalk" or "Sand in My Shoes"? When it came to the Drifters, Weiss said, "At that point, 'Under the Boardwalk' was almost a current. That phrase 'beach music' really meant those *old* songs. Some of that music wasn't old enough. That stuff wasn't beach music yet....The old Clyde McPhatter Drifters and those old '50s songs—*that* was beach music." He also noted that a song's obscurity didn't mean it wouldn't be included, which of course eventually became a given when classifying something as beach music. ""Zing' for example, wasn't a Coasters *hit*, but it was a big beach song," he said.

Having secured permissions and everything else they needed, Weiss and Atlantic decided to put out an album, and started something that—with a few fits and starts—would become a full-blown industry in less than twenty years.

BEACH BEAT (ATLANTIC RECORDS 8140, 1967)

Side 1
1. The Clovers, "One Mint Julep"
2. The Coasters, "Zing! Went the Strings of My Heart"
3. Barbara Lewis, "Think a Little Sugar"
4. Chuck Willis, "C.C. Rider"
5. Clyde McPhatter & the Drifters, "Money Honey"
6. Willie Tee, "Walking Up a One Way Street"

Side 2
1. The Drifters, "There Goes My Baby"
2. Doris Troy, "Just One Look"
3. The Coasters, "Searchin'"

4. "Stick" McGhee, "Drinkin' Wine, Spo-Dee-O-Dee"
5. Willie Tee, "Thank You John"
6. Clyde McPhatter & the Drifters, "Honey Love"

The Songs

Since this album contains two songs by the Coasters and Willie Tee and three by the Drifters, the track listings cover the main elements of the artists' biography up until the release of the track and then pick the back story up again on the write-up for the artists' next track.

Side 1
1. "One Mint Julep" | The Clovers (1952)

The Clovers formed in Washington, D.C., around 1946 as the 4 Clovers, and after several years and a few unsuccessful small-label recordings, they eventually got an audition with Ahmet Ertegun of the up-and-coming Atlantic label. In 1951, they signed with Atlantic, and their first two single releases, "Don't You Know I Love You" and "Fool, Fool, Fool," both went to #1 on the R&B charts. Suddenly, the group was in great demand, frequently playing at the Apollo Theater and even appearing on the cover of *Cash Box* magazine.

In late 1951, they recorded some new songs at Atlantic studios, among them "One Mint Julep," which was released in 1952. Recorded with Buddy Bailey singing lead, its release followed "Stick" McGhee's "Drinkin' Wine Spo-Dee-O-Dee" (see side 2) by a few years, but "One Mint Julep" kicked off a somewhat sustained series of "drinking-story songs" that would hit the airwaves in the early '50s. As the story of a man who ended up married all because of "One Mint Julep," it's a humorous take on the evils of drink. The singer and a

woman he meets have a few "nips," and one thing leads to another and the singer tells us getting "frisky" ended up saddling him with six extra children! "One Mint Julep" was a hit, peaking at #2 on the R&B charts. The song would be covered by several other artists, and in 1961, Ray Charles's version would go to #1 on the R&B charts.

After "One Mint Julep," the Clovers released six more singles from 1952 through 1954, and every one of them made the Top 10 on the R&B charts. The group was recognized as one of the biggest acts in the music business, and by 1953, they had topped two million in record sales. They released the iconic beach song "Nip Sip" (see *Beach Beat Vol. 2*) in 1955 and would have three more Top 10 hits in 1956. The Clovers garnered an astounding twenty-one chart records and a legacy as a seminal rock and R&B group. From the earliest days of beach music, the Clovers' recordings have been an essential part of the beach music canon. In a genre where musical tastes and standards have fluctuated considerably over the course of seven-plus decades, the Clovers are one of a few groups who have remained relevant and continue to hold an iconic status in the oeuvre.

2. "Zing! Went the Strings of My Heart" | The Coasters (1958)

The Coasters had their origins in the 1940s in a variety of groups with ever-changing memberships who sang under several different names before 1955. As the Robins, they recorded a Jerry Leiber and Mike Stoller song called "Riot in Cell Block #9" on their Spark label, but it didn't have an impact on the charts. Leiber and Stoller sold the label to Atlantic, and at that point

the group fractured and some members formed the Coasters and were signed to Atlantic's then-new Atco label.

They first charted with "Down in Mexico," which kicked off a long string of sustained chart hits when it went to #8 on the R&B charts in 1956. In 1957, "Young Blood" also went to #8, while its flip side, "Searchin'," did even better by charting at #3. They recorded "Yakety Yak," a #1 smash, in 1958, and while

"Yakety Yak" was wowing crowds, some listeners flipped the 45 over and found an excellent version of "Zing! Went the Strings of My Heart." As a cover of an old standard written by songwriter James Hanley in 1935, Judy Garland's 1939 recording was probably the most famous version, though artists such as Frank Sinatra and Dinah Shore had recorded it as well. The real anomaly concerning the record, though, is that it was unlike the Coasters' hits up to that point. The three songs the group charted with in 1957, the year before "Zing!" was released, were "Young Blood," "Searchin'" and "Idol with the Golden Head," and clearly what audiences expected from the Coasters were the "novelty" or "storytelling" hits for which they were famous. This may explain why a quality recording such as "Zing!" went unnoticed by many listeners at the time, in that perhaps this love song with a doo-wop feel was so atypical for Coasters listeners that it just didn't register. Producers Leiber and Stoller reportedly considered it the greatest doo-wop song ever recorded, but when I interviewed the Coasters' last surviving original member Carl Gardner in 2010, he didn't think a lot of the song, telling me only that the song's appeal was due mainly to the bass singing of "Will 'Dub' Jones, who was one of the best." Beach music audiences, however, loved it.

The Coasters' story continues on side 2 with the entry for "Searchin',"

3. "Think a Little Sugar" | Barbara Lewis (1963)

Barbara Lewis was born to musical parents who both played instruments and performed when Lewis was a child. She started writing music when she was nine, and in high school she competed in a talent show that brought her to attention of disc jockey and producer Ollie McLaughlin, who mentored her and arranged for her to cut her first record, a regional hit she had written called "My Heart Went Do Dat Da," in 1962. McLaughlin worked out a deal with Chess Records to get Lewis some studio time and even arranged for Lewis to arrive a day early to see Etta James

recording. The next day, Lewis recorded a song she had written herself called "Hello Stranger," which would be her first hit. Released on Atlantic in 1963, "Hello Stranger" rose to #3 on the pop charts and went to #1 on the R&B charts. Perhaps surprisingly, though, "Hello Stranger" was a hit on the beach music circuit, but the flip side of the record, "Think a Little Sugar," is probably bigger. Recorded with the Dells on backup, this song gives the single a one-two punch that is perhaps unparalleled in the beach music milieu. As a flip side, "Think a Little Sugar" did not chart, but it has remained a popular beach song nonetheless.

Lewis would go on to have a number of big hits for Atlantic, including "Baby I'm Yours" and "Make Me Your Baby." She eventually left the recording industry, and by the early '70s, she had pursued other jobs unrelated to the music business. In the 1990s, Lewis started performing once again; she received the Pioneer Award from the Rhythm and Blues Foundation in 1999.

4. "C.C. Rider" | Chuck Willis (1957)

Harold "Chuck" Willis signed with Columbia Records in 1951, and in 1956, he moved to Atlantic. Willis had a number of chart records during his brief recording career (he died of peritonitis at the age of thirty-two), including "It's Too Late," "What Am I Living For" and "Hang Up My Rock and Roll Shoes." His biggest hit, however, was "C.C. Rider" in 1957, and despite the fact that Willis was a prolific writer, it's one of only a few songs he recorded that he didn't write. Originally recorded as "See See Rider" by Gertrude "Ma" Rainey in 1924, the song about an unfaithful lover had been recorded by Jelly Roll Morton, Big Bill Broonzy, Lead Belly and Blind Lemon Jefferson. A version by Wee Bea Booze in 1943 hit #1 on the Harlem Hit Parade chart.

Willis's version of "C.C. Rider" was #1 on the R&B charts in 1957, and he would have one other #1 hit, "What Am I Living For," which hit #1 on the R&B charts a month after his death. Yet despite its success, "C.C. Rider" is possibly the only song on this album that has not aged well in terms of beach music popularity. Based on Ed Weiss's observations, "C.C. Rider" may have been popular at the time and/or demand may have been high for the song, but in any event, it was not a song that would be found on another beach music compilation album within the scope of this book. Perhaps because the song is a bit too slow, it is not a sought-after song by beach music lovers or even fans of shag music today.

5. "Money Honey" | Clyde McPhatter & the Drifters (1953)

The Drifters got their start when Clyde McPhatter left Billy Ward and the Dominoes in 1953, and Ahmet Ertegun of Atlantic Records urged him to form his own group. McPhatter first assembled the members of a gospel group he had worked with, but Ertegun was disappointed with the results and told McPhatter to put together an entirely different group. This time McPhatter recruited South Carolina–born Bill Pinkney, brothers Andrew and Gerhart Thrasher, Willie Ferbee and Walter Adams. When this group emerged from the studio, Atlantic was pleased with the results, and released "Money Honey" in 1953. The song is about a man who needs money to pay his rent and asks his favorite girl for some "Money, honey." The song, which the label credited to Clyde McPhatter and the Drifters, went to #1 on the R&B charts, and the group was on its way.

McPhatter sang lead on several more hits, including the beach music classic "Honey Love," (see side 2) which topped the R&B charts and went to #21 on the pop charts before McPhatter was drafted and sold his controlling share of the group to manager George Treadwell. At that point, the group's lineup changed again, as will be discussed in the write-up for "There Goes My Baby" on side 2.

6. "Walking Up a One Way Street" | Willie Tee (1965)

Willie Tee was born Wilson Turbinton in New Orleans, where he was surrounded and influenced by the vibrant New Orleans music scene. Willie and his brother put together their first band, which played local gigs and even cut a demo. According to Fensterstock, in junior high, Willie's music teacher was none other than Harold Batiste, who in 1961 would form the first all-Black-owned record label in New Orleans, A.F.O. (All For One), along with New Orleans music scene luminaries such as Allen Toussaint and Melvin Lastie. As a producer and arranger for the label, Batiste worked on now-

legendary songs such as Barbara George's "I Know," Joe Jones's "You Talk Too Much," Lee Dorsey's "Ya Ya" and others. In 1962, Turbinton, though still in high school, recorded his first single, "Always Accused," on A.F.O. Although the song got some airplay locally, it is only notable in that the recording was attributed to Willie Tee, a name given to Turbinton by A.F.O.'s house saxophonist Red Tyler. He recorded one more single on A.F.O. before the label folded and then recorded on the Cinderella label, but none of his songs were hits.

Tee next signed with his cousin Julius Gaines's New Orleans–based Nola records. The label's eighth single release was "Teasin' You," and the song quickly found a regional audience. Atlantic picked up the rights to distribute the song nationally, and it just barely charted at #97, though it did reach #12 on the R&B charts. Almost unnoticed was the flip side of the record, the now popular "Walking Up a One Way Street." That song, in which Tee laments being left alone and almost tortured by his lover, puts into perspective the one-sidedness of their relationship. Plaintive and soulful, Tee's song, though it did not chart, nevertheless touched a nerve with beach music lovers and has remained a classic since its release. Like many beach music songs, its failure to make the national charts has not been an impediment to its popularity.

The Top 100 *Billboard* slot "Teasin' You" earned was apparently encouraging enough that Atlantic gave Tee another shot, and his next recording for the label was 1965's immortal "Thank You John." Tee's story, and the story of "Thank You John," will be continued on side 2.

Side 2
1. "There Goes My Baby" | The Drifters (1959)

After the early success of the Drifters under Clyde McPhatter, no doubt there was concern about how well his replacement, Johnny Moore, would fare. Moore joined the group and took over as lead singer, and in fact, he performed so well on subsequent recordings that it takes a very sophisticated listener to discern that it isn't still McPhatter singing lead. Their first recording with Moore as lead was "Adorable," which went to #1 on the R&B charts and was followed by several chart records, including the classic "Ruby Baby," which their first collaboration with producers Jerry Leiber and Mike Stoller, who also wrote the song. But there were further personnel changes, and soon Moore was drafted; due to personal problems, shortly thereafter Atlantic fired the rest of the group.

Atlantic knew that the Drifters' name was a valuable commodity that shouldn't be wasted, and they had previously heard a young singer named Benjamin Nelson (later to become Ben E. King) singing with his group the Five Crowns. Atlantic hired Nelson and his group to become the new Drifters, and their first release was "There Goes My Baby," which went to #2 on the charts and had the distinction of being one of the first rock records to incorporate strings. Still working with Leiber and Stoller, this would be the most successful phase of the group's chart history. While the earlier Drifters' music had more of a doo-wop feel, the new Drifters music had a more elegant sound, and the #1 hit "Save the Last Dance for Me," written by the famous songwriting team Doc Pomus and Mort Shuman, seemed to confirm that they'd found the right formula. Other songs from this period included "Dance with Me," "I Count the Tears"and "This Magic Moment," another Pomus and Shuman composition.

Not long after this, Nelson, now going by Ben E. King, left for a solo career, and the Drifters' lineup changed several times and saw a variety of singers doing lead duties. Over the course of the next four years, with four different lead singers, many songs that were hits on the pop charts also became beach standards, including "Save the Last Dance for Me" (#1, 1960), "Up on the Roof" (#5, 1962), and of course two of the most popular beach hits ever, "Under the Boardwalk" (#4, 1964) and "I've Got Sand in My Shoes" (#33, 1964). There were many more as well.

Their last song to make the U.S. charts was in 1966, and they left Atlantic Records and headed to England, which was gripped in the northern soul boom. They signed with Bell Records, where they'd have great chart success all over again, with songs that have since become anthologized beach music classics such as "Kissin' in the Back Row" and "(You're More than a Number in) My Little Red Book" and others.

2. "Just One Look" | Doris Troy (1963)

Born Doris Elaine Higgenson in New York City, Doris Troy got her start in the music business working as an usher at the Apollo Theater at age sixteen. At the Apollo she was reportedly discovered by James Brown, and her first active role as a singer was as a part of the Gospelaires (with Dionne and Dee Dee Warwick). She recorded a solo side as Doris Payne (her grandmother's surname) in 1960, followed by duets on small labels with Doc Bagby, as half of Jay and Dee and with Pearl Woods.

She was also writing, and her song "How About That" was a hit for Dee Clark in 1960. But it was when she recorded a demo of her own song "Just One Look" that everything changed. Atlantic's Jerry Wexler loved it so much that they released it straight off the demo she'd made without rerecording it, although she did change her name again, this time to Doris Troy in honor of Helen of Troy. The single raced to #10 on the pop charts and became a bona fide hit, but she would never have another Top 40 or even Top 100 pop or R&B hit in America. However, several of her songs became smashes in England, and she was so much more successful in England that she moved there in the late 1960s. In 1969, she signed with Apple Records, which would allow her to work with Beatles George Harrison and Ringo Starr.

She cut a few singles in the 1970s, but she also started session work as a background singer. She sang on a number of famous recordings, including the Rolling Stones' "You Can't Always Get What You Want," and along with Clare Torry she provided the haunting backing vocals on the 1973 Pink Floyd album *Dark Side of the Moon*. Other artists she performed backup work for during her career included Dusty Springfield, Jackie Wilson, Chuck Jackson, the Drifters, James Brown, Tom Jones and many others. In the 1980s, *Mama, I Want to Sing!*, a musical based on her life, ran for 1,500 performances off Broadway and was eventually made into a film. She died in Las Vegas in 2004.

3. "Searchin'" | The Coasters (1957)

Although "Zing!" by the Coasters appears first on this album, "Searchin'," another Jerry Leiber and Mike Stoller composition, was actually released first, in March 1957. "Searchin'" tells of a man who will use detectives such as Sherlock Holmes, Charlie Chan, Joe Friday, Sam Spade and Bulldog Drummond to find his lost love. (Beach music lovers may recognize that 1963's "Kidnapper," by Jewell and the Rubies, uses a similar scenario, mentioning '60s legal and detective shows.) "Searchin'" was #1 on the R&B chart for twelve weeks, but it also hit #3 on the pop charts. Interestingly, the B side of the single was "Young Blood," which also went to #1 on the R&B chart and reached #8 on the pop charts.

Oddly enough, while the Coasters followed this double-sided hit with now-famous chart records such as "Idol with the Golden Head," "Yakety Yak," "Charlie Brown" and "Poison Ivy," all of those songs peaked by August 1959. By the early 1960s, their doo-wop novelty songs were becoming somewhat passé, and after 1961, they charted only twice more. In beach music circles, however, songs such as "Zing!" and "Searchin'" have become time-tested classics.

4. "Drinkin' Wine, Spo-Dee-O-Dee" | "Stick" McGhee (1949)

Granville Henry "Stick" McGhee was not a drummer, as some might think given his nickname, but a guitar player and a singer. His nickname wasn't "Sticks," plural, either, but "Stick," and Stick got his nickname by pushing his polio-stricken brother Walter "Brownie" McGhee around in a wagon with a stick when they were children. After his discharge from the military in 1946, Stick, along with Brownie and friend Dan Burley, laid down a track Stick used to sing in the army, retitled "Drinkin' Wine Spo-Dee-O-Dee" on Mayo Williams' small Harlem Label (Spo-dee-o-dee is reported to be the leftovers and dregs of many wine bottles, poured together and passed around). However, Stick's army version had been quite different and quite profane, so it was a drastically sanitized and slower version that was released for radio play. The song did not sell well and did not chart.

As Gillett also notes in *Making Tracks*, Ahmet Ertegun, one of the founders of Atlantic Records, heard about the song and was told that it was getting significant airplay in New Orleans. Ertegun got hold of a copy and liked it, so in February 1949 he tracked down Stick and, with Brownie on guitar and "Big Chief" Ellis on piano, had them rerecord it with a new, more up-tempo rhythm.

26

The record was Atlantic's first big hit, going all the way to #2 on the R&B charts and #26 on the pop charts, a rare crossover hit for a Black artist in the early 1950s. McGhee followed up with several singles, but only 1951's "Tennessee Waltz Blues" charted, going to #2 on the R&B charts, though it did not register on the pop charts.

After a few more releases, McGhee left Atlantic records for King, where he recorded as "Sticks" McGhee and cut such living-on-the-edge jump-blues singles as "Whiskey, Women and Loaded Dice," "Jungle Juice" and "Dealin' from the Bottom." McGhee later moved to Savoy records, but further chart success was elusive. He died in 1961.

5. "Thank You John" | Willie Tee (1965)

Willie Tee had started recording for labels such as A.F.O., Cinderella and Nola records before "Teasin' You" was picked up by Atlantic. Even though sales weren't impressive, Atlantic gave Willie Tee another shot, and his next recording for the label was 1965's immortal "Thank You John."

"Thank You John" is an odd song, or at least the subject matter is. It seems to be about deception, infidelity, physical abuse, pimping, lying— any and all of the above. Though "Thank You John" failed to connect with fans nationally, it was popular enough that Tee began touring on the famed "Chitlin Circuit." Despite a failure to consistently connect with fans nationally, in the Southeast the record became a beach music staple in a very short time indeed.

After "Thank You John" and his next single both failed to chart, Tee wasn't

asked to renew his contract with Atlantic. His next single was for Nola, 1966's great "Please Don't Go," now regarded as a good beach tune in its own right. Of his subsequent singles on Nola, Hot Line, Bonatemp and even Capitol, none really did much outside of the New Orleans area. He created his own label, Gatur, with old friend Julius Gaines in 1971. Tee released singles on the label throughout the decade, and he remained a mainstay of the

New Orleans music scene, performing, producing and recording a variety of music until his death in 2007.

6. "Honey Love" | Clyde McPhatter & the Drifters (1954)

With Clyde McPhatter singing lead on "Money Honey," the Drifters had their first big hit when it went to #1 on the R&B charts in 1953. McPhatter sang lead on several more hits, including "Such a Night" (#2 R&B charts, 1954), "Bip Bam" (#7 R&B charts, 1954) and "White Christmas" (#2 R&B charts, 1954) and in all, they had five Top 10 R&B hits in 1954, including "Honey Love."

According to Charlie Gillett, both "White Christmas" and "Honey Love" were all recorded in the same three-hour session. It was apparently the group's first brush with controversy as well. Censorship was strict during the 1950s, and even somewhat innocuous songs such as the Everly Brothers' "Wake Up Little Susie," Hank Ballard's "Work with Me, Annie" and even thirteen-year-old Jimmy Boyd's version of "I Saw Mommy Kissing Santa Claus" were banned from the radio for "suggestiveness." In the case of "Honey Love," written by McPhatter and Jerry Wexler, authorities in Memphis took offense with McPhatter singing that he needed and wanted "it," although one would have to put the worst possible spin on the lyrics to get only something suggestive from "it." Nevertheless, WDIA in Memphis took the song off its playlists, and Memphis police apparently confiscated copies of the record so they couldn't be played on jukeboxes. Banning "Honey Love" didn't hurt sales nationally, however, and it was the group's second R&B #1. It stayed there for eight weeks.

It was at this time that McPhatter was drafted and sold his controlling share of the group to manager George Treadwell. As successful as the group had been, their greatest success was still ahead.

2

UNFINISHED BUSINESS:
BEACH BEAT VOL. 2

ATLANTIC RECORDS 8191, 1968

*O*ne year after the release of *Beach Beat*, Atlantic rolled out a follow-up called *Beach Beat Vol. 2*. "*Beach Beat* did well enough—it sold at least ten thousand albums—but I don't remember how many exactly. But it sold enough for them to do another one," Ed Weiss told me. "And since the first one did well enough to try a second one, *Beach Beat Volume 2* was the result." After never having a compilation album to listen to, beach music lovers must have been thrilled to have a second album come out a year later. It seemed to suggest endless possibilities—and in a way, it did.

The first problem Weiss said he and Atlantic faced, however, was what songs to include this time around. "Atlantic has such as vast catalogue, but we had kind of run through the high-demand stuff on Atlantic. There was some, but there wasn't enough to do a whole album. But I also had some friends at Chess Records, and so we had licensing for some of the Chess songs. We were able to get those songs on the second one." On this album, in addition

to Atlantic standards by Willie Tee, the Clovers, Barbara Lewis and others, songs from the Chess catalogue by Bobby Moore & the Rhythm Aces, Billy Stewart and Tony Clarke filled out the bulk of the album and were arguably the albums' best tracks. Weiss even secured "May I" by Maurice Williams and the Zodiacs from Dee-Su Records, a song that had not been a chart hit but that was popular in the beach clubs in the Carolinas and Virginia.

This album is probably better overall than the first one, especially because of the Chess and Dee-Su selections. But "Memphis Soul Stew" is marginal, "Without Love (There Is Nothing)" is weak and nothing would bring a beach party to more of a screeching halt than "I (Who Have Nothing)." Again, it's easy to pass judgment five decades later, but it's interesting to note that for all the various artist beach albums that have come out since 1968, those three songs have never again been included on a beach music compilation album.

In the end, Weiss said, "It didn't sell as well as the first one, but it did well enough." Chris Beachley said he thought it was because the second album "was good, but not quite as good as the first one." In any event, it would be the last Atlantic *Beach Beat* album.

BEACH BEAT VOL. 2 (ATLANTIC RECORDS 8191, 1968)

Side 1
1. Bobby Moore & the Rhythm Aces, "Searching for My Love"
2. Willie Tee, "Teasin' You"
3. Barbara Lewis, "Hello Stranger"
4. Billy Stewart, "Fat Boy"
5. King Curtis & the Kingpins, "Memphis Soul Stew"
6. Maurice Williams & the Zodiacs, "May I"

Side 2
1. Lenny O'Henry, "Across the Street"
2. Clyde McPhatter, "Without Love (There Is Nothing)"
3. The Coasters, "Idol with the Golden Head"
4. Tony Clarke, "The Entertainer"
5. The Clovers, "Nip Sip"
6. Ben E. King, "I (Who Have Nothing)"

Unlike the first collection, this album had liner notes.

> Beach Beat Volume 2! *More of the music enjoyed every summer by swingers from coast to coast. The beach itself means different things to different people, but the beat of the beach is universal. It starts with the cry "Let's have a party," and from then on, the twenty-four-hour excitement is accented by and depends upon the beat of the beach. But all too soon, vacation is over and it's time to return home. However, the beat of the beach lives on in the songs of the summer, found first in* Beach Beat, Volume One, *and now in this album.*

The notes go on to say, "In choosing the songs for this album, we tried to find the ones most requested in record stores, and at radio stations; the songs most popular, and yet hardest to find." Finally, they thank "the WKIX Music Men (Raleigh, NC)—Russ Spooner, Bob Jones, Tommy Walker, John Stanton, Charlie Brown, Tom Scott, Marc Starr."

The Songs

Side 1
1. "Searching for My Love" | Bobby Moore & the Rhythm Aces (1966)

New Orleans–born Robert "Bobby" Moore's first experience in a group came when he was serving in the army in the early 1950s. A tenor sax player, his first group consisted of members of the Fort Benning, Georgia army marching band. After leaving the army, he decided to make music his profession and formed the Rhythm Aces in 1961. As a unit, the Rhythm Aces quickly gained a reputation as a first-class ensemble, and as a result, they had the opportunity to back up singers such as Ray Charles, Sam and Dave, Etta James, Wilson Pickett, Sam Cooke and Otis Redding.

They didn't want to be just a backup band, however, and in 1965, they got their first real shot as a feature act at the legendary Muscle Shoals Studio in Alabama. There they recorded "Searching for My Love," which Moore himself had written. "We were playing the song in clubs for a long time before we ever recorded it, and decided it would be a good one to record because people liked it when we played it—I think the response there had a lot to do with it," bandmember

Bobby Moore Jr. told me. "We went to Muscle Shoals and were one of the first Chess groups to record there. We cut the record, and it took off." Chess Records picked up the tune and released it on their Checker label in 1966, and the group watched the song soar into the pop Top 40 before finally settling in at #27, where it eventually sold more than one million copies.

After "Searching for My Love" the group was hot and even performed on television's *Where the Action Is* as a follow-up to the single. They were hoping their next release would sustain that momentum, and though "Try My Love Again" is a solid beach music classic, it peaked at #97 and #40 on the R&B charts. Their next single did not make the pop Top 100 at all, and despite the promise shown by the Rhythm Aces' early singles, Checker didn't seem to have much faith in the group's ability to produce long term. After they released two more non-charting singles, the label dropped them.

Bobby Moore Sr. died in 2006, but his son kept the band going. Considering that they cut only five singles, having had two emerge as sizeable beach music classics is a testimony to the quality of their music, even if their limited chart success means they aren't as well known today as some other national acts from the period.

2. "Teasin' You" | Willie Tee (1965)

Willie Tee had two songs featured on the first *Beach Beat* album, but perhaps what is most interesting is that the biggest chart hit he ever had was this song, though it was *not* covered on the first *Beach Beat* album, passed over instead for "Thank You John" and "Walking Up a One Way Street." The fact is that while those two songs are considered beach music classics, "Teasin' You" makes the cut as a beach song mainly on the backs of those two selections and Willie Tee's reputation in beach music circles.

Nevertheless, after Tee signed with New Orleans–based Nola records, "Teasin' You" was recorded and released and became popular regionally. Oddly enough, Tee had been reluctant to record it because he felt it was too great a departure from the jazz-like sound he was seeking to be known for. After the Righteous Brothers sang "Teasin' You" on the popular music showcase program *Shindig!*, suddenly Tee was a hot property. Atlantic picked up the rights to distribute the song nationally, and while it just barely charted at #97 on the pop charts, it did reach #12 on the R&B charts.

Atlantic decided to release another Willie Tee single after the moderate success of "Teasin' You," but as recounted in chapter 1, his next recording for the label was 1965's "Thank You John." It was not a hit, and after one more Atlantic release did nothing, Atlantic dropped him, though he did get one last shot on Atco. Releases on Nola, Hot Line, Bonatemp, Capitol and his own Gatur label didn't do anything nationally, nor did releases on a half-dozen other labels, including Polydor and United Artists. He remained immensely popular on the New Orleans music scene for the rest of his life, however, performing, producing and recording a variety of music until his death in 2007.

3. "Hello Stranger" | Barbara Lewis (1963)

Like Willie Tee, Barbara Lewis also had a song on the first *Beach Beat* album, and interestingly enough, it was "Think a Little Sugar," the B side of this record. As the write-up for "Think a Little Sugar" explains in chapter 1, Lewis came to the attention of disc jockey and producer Ollie McLaughlin, who mentored her and arranged for her to cut her first record in 1962 on the Karen label. McLaughlin then worked out a deal with Chicago's Chess Records to get Lewis some studio time, and she recorded a song she had written herself called "Hello Stranger," the single that would be her first hit. Lewis claimed that idea for the record came from touring with her father, and people would tell him, "Hello Stranger…it's been a long time."

McLaughlin was able to get the Dells, who recorded for the Chess subsidiary Argo, to do the "chew-bop, chew-bop, my baby" background vocals on Lewis's record. With the five Dells and Lewis in the recording booth at the same time crowded around two microphones, after thirteen takes they felt they had a winner, so much so that the Dells' Chuck Barksdale was telling Lewis and the others, "It's a hit, it's a hit." McLaughlin thought so too, as he went to New York and sold "Hello Stranger" and some other sides to Atlantic. Atlantic wasn't as sure about "Hello Stranger" as McLaughlin was, but when they released "Hello Stranger," it rose to #3 in the summer of 1963 and went to #1 on the R&B charts.

Two of Lewis's next four singles on Atlantic would break the Top 100, but it was 1965's Van McCoy–produced "Baby I'm Yours" that would be her next standout hit. The single went to #11 on the pop 100 and #5 on the R&B charts, and her next single, "Make Me Your Baby," would rise as high as its predecessor, #11 on the pop charts and #9 on the R&B charts. Lewis would have just one more pop Top 40 hit, "Make Me Belong to You," which would peak at #28 and would also find an audience in beach music and northern soul circles. After a string of subsequent non-charting singles, in the 1970s, Lewis pursued other jobs unrelated to the music business.

4. "Fat Boy" | Billy Stewart (1962)

Born William Larry Stewart, "Billy" Stewart was involved in music at an early age as a member of his family's group, the Stewart Gospel Singers. He won a talent show singing the George Gershwin tune "Summertime" when he was a teenager, but his first real break came in 1955 when Bo Diddley heard his piano playing skills and asked him to join his band. Stewart recorded his first song, "Billy's Blues," with Diddley on guitar on Chess in 1956. Though the record met with some success, it wasn't a national hit, nor were subsequent singles, and Stewart spent the next five years as a background singer and player with Diddley.

Chess hired a new A&R man, Roquel Davis, and he encouraged Stewart to record solo once again. His first recording was 1962's "Reap What You Sow," which went to #18 on the R&B charts and #79 on the *Billboard* Hot 100. The flip side of the record was a song Davis had asked Stewart to write and record based on his nickname, "Fat Boy." This song exists in two versions: the original mono version starts with a guitar

and a calliope opening the record (this is the version on *Beach Beat Vol. 2*) while the stereo version features the guitar only. Though "Fat Boy" did not chart, it got a fair amount of airplay and would become Stewart's signature song.

He had his first really big hit in 1965 with a song he had written called "I Do Love You," which went to #6 on the R&B charts and #26 on the pop Top 40 and stayed on the charts for twenty-one weeks. Subsequent releases included "Sitting in the Park," which went to #4 on the R&B charts and #24 on the pop Top 40. Stewart had eight subsequent pop Top 100 releases, including a version of George Gershwin's "Summertime" that hit #10 on the pop Top 40 in 1966. Several other releases did moderately well, but his weight was causing increasing problems, he developed diabetes, and in 1969 he had a motorcycle accident. In January 1970, Stewart was killed while on tour when the car he and three band members were in plunged off a bridge near Smithfield, North Carolina. He was just thirty-two years old.

5. "Memphis Soul Stew" | King Curtis & the Kingpins (1967)

Born as Curtis Ousley in Fort Worth, Texas, by the age of twelve he could play alto saxophone and acoustic guitar, and in fact he was proficient at many instruments. When he was nineteen, he was invited by conductor Lionel Leo Hampton to play with his orchestra in New York, and his career kicked in after that. Now known as "King Curtis," he worked as a session musician for a variety of labels, perhaps most famously for Atco/Atlantic, where he played saxophone on several of the Coasters' biggest hits. Larkin notes that he had his own #1 R&B hit in 1962, "Soul Twist," on the Enjoy label, and then signed with Capitol, where he had the #20 R&B hit "Soul Serenade." He signed with Atco in 1965, and his second chart release there was a song he wrote called "Memphis Soul Stew." The song has a funky beat, and Curtis calls for instruments like the bass, drums and horns, to come in a half teacup, pound or tablespoons at a time, as if the song is a recipe. The song went to #6 in 1967, and Curtis would have a dozen Top 100 pop hits at Atco up until 1971. Over the course of his career, he worked with artists such as Jimi Hendrix, Bobby Darin, Aretha Franklin, Sam Cooke, John Lennon, and others. Curtis and his group the Kingpins opened for the Beatles at Shea Stadium in 1965, and in 1970 he won a Grammy for Best R&B Instrumental Performance. Unfortunately, he was just thirty-seven years old when he was murdered during an argument in 1971.

While King Curtis is without a doubt one of the most acclaimed artists in this book, "Memphis Soul Stew" is not generally now considered a beach song. It's surprising that a song that had peaked on the charts just months before the release of this album would be included when there was supposedly a deliberate effort to exclude newer music on the Atlantic albums. One wonders if the label pushed to include the song because it was riding a wave of popularity at the time, because the song's closest connection to beach music might be as a solid party song.

6. "May I" | Maurice Williams and the Zodiacs (1967)

Lancaster, South Carolina native Maurice Williams started singing in church when he was just six years old, and by the early 1950s he had formed a group and was writing songs. In 1956, he headed to Nashville, where he and his group—recently re-christened the Gladiolas—recorded a song he'd written in 1953 called "Little Darling." The song was released on the Excello label and reached #41 on the pop charts and #11 on the R&B charts (Williams authorized a version that the white cover group the Diamonds did, which went to no 2 on the pop charts—and paid him royalties). After a few more singles, the group left Excello, yet again changing their name, this time to the Zodiacs. In 1960, they signed with Herald Records in New York and recorded another song Williams had written, "Stay," which reached #1.

Five Herald singles followed, and the group left Herald after 1962 and started label jumping before ending up with Vee Jay, where in 1965 they recorded "May I." The label was in serious financial trouble at the time and declared bankruptcy, and as a result, "May I" probably didn't get promoted like it should have. Williams had faith in the record, however, and he contacted Marshall Sehorn and Allen Toussaint and arranged for the song to be rereleased on their New Orleans–based Dee-Su label in 1967. It still wasn't a national hit, but it became one of the greatest beach music classics of all time, even more so than "Stay." It was a favorite all along the East Coast and was so popular that Bill Deal and the Rhondels recorded it and had a Top 40 hit with it in 1969. As Ammon Tharp of the Rhondels

told me, "We played down in the Carolinas, and during the summer of 1968 people kept requesting 'May I'....We'd get requests to do it two or three times a night. We came back home to Virginia Beach and said, 'Wow—we really gotta record this damn thing.'" Amazingly, although "May I" never charted for the Zodiacs, due largely to the beach music and R&B crowds in the South, it would sell over one million copies over the years and earn a gold record as well.

Side 2
1. "Across the Street" | Lenny O'Henry (1963)

Buffalo, New York native Danny Cannon began his career as a founding member of the Vibra-Harps in 1955, and along with Donnie Elbert, Charles Hargro and Donald Simmons, the group recorded their first single for the Beech label in 1958. Elbert soon left the group and went on to find fame as a songwriter ("Open the Door to Your Heart" for Darrell Banks) and performer in his own right, with four Top 100 singles. In the meantime, the remaining group members recorded several singles, but failing to find any sustainable success, the group broke up and reunited several times.

On one occasion when they re-formed, they signed with ABC-Paramount. ABC apparently decided that Cannon should be billed as frontman, his name should be Lenny O'Henry and the backing group (the Vibraharps) would be called the Short Stories. After one single, Cannon went out on his own as Lenny O'Henry and signed with Atco in 1963. In 1964, he released "Across the Street," his claim to beach music fame. He had worked with Bob Crewe on his last ABC single, and by 1964, Crewe was working with the Four Seasons, who had already had three #1 hits produced and co-written by Crewe and Bob Gaudio.

Reconnecting with his old friend, "Across the Street" was co-written by Crewe and Charlie Calello, who arranged many of the Four Seasons' big hits as well as "Across the Street." As a further bonus, Crewe and Calello were able to get the Four

Seasons to do the male backing vocals. The song was a fantastic recording, but unfortunately the recording barely registered nationally. The single stalled at #98 during its one-week stay on the charts and then disappeared from sight. Even so, in his book *The Heart of Rock & Soul: The 1001 Greatest Singles Ever Made*, rock critic Dave Marsh lists "Across the Street" at #782—not a bad all-time listing for a record that was under the radar nationally.

Sadly, it would be O'Henry's most successful record, though not for lack of effort by Crewe and company. Even with the hottest producing, writing and arranging ensemble in the business, O'Henry's subsequent records didn't chart. Even a 1967 re-release of "Across the Street" didn't fare as well as it had the first time. O'Henry retired from the music business and died in 2014.

"Across the Street" has the distinction of being the only song to appear on an Atlantic *Beach Beat* album in the '60s, the first *Billy Smith's Beach Party* album in the late '70s and the first *Ocean Drive* album and the first Ripete *Beach Beat* album in 1980; it's also on the *It Will Stand* list of the greatest beach music hits of all time. That's quite an accomplishment for a song that barely cracked the Top 100, but it is a testament to its greatness.

2. "Without Love (There Is Nothing)" | Clyde McPhatter (1957)

Clyde Lensley McPhatter was born in Durham, North Carolina, and after his family moved to New York City, he joined the Mount Lebanon Singers of the Mount Lebanon Church. Although Mount Lebanon's was one of the most popular gospel groups on the East Coast, McPhatter's interests eventually moved him toward rhythm and blues, and he entered an amateur contest at the Apollo Theater. There he was spotted by Billy Ward, who was forming a new singing group. In 1950, McPhatter joined Ward, Charlie White, Bill Brown, and Joe Lamont to form the Dominoes, and while it was Brown's bass voice that was featured on their early smash "Sixty Minute Man," soon it was McPhatter's voice that was attracting the notice.

By 1953, McPhatter had left the Dominoes and signed with Atlantic in May of that year, becoming the lead of the Drifters. With McPhatter's distinctive voice singing lead, the group reeled off a series of hits, including "Money Honey" and "Honey Love," before McPhatter was drafted and sold his controlling share of the group to manager George Treadwell. When he was discharged in 1955, he returned to Atlantic as a solo act, although his first recording was a duet with Ruth Brown, "Love Has Joined Us Together." On his own in 1956, he released "Seven Days" (pop #44, R&B #2), "Treasure of Love" (pop #16, R&B #1) and "Without Love (There Is Nothing)" (pop #19, R&B #4). "Without Love (There Is Nothing)" was better suited for slow dancing than shagging, but the song has been quite highly regarded outside of beach music circles. Throughout the years, the song has been recorded by a number of artists, and Tom Jones's 1969 version was the most successful, hitting #5 on the pop charts and going all the way to #1 on the Easy Listening chart. Ray Charles, Little Richard, Elvis Presley and others recorded the song as well.

McPhatter still had some big songs ahead of him, such as 1958's "A Lover's Question," but by 1960, fewer and fewer of his singles were charting. He left Atlantic, moved to MGM and then signed with Mercury. His releases on Mercury were hit and miss, some not charting at all, and others, such as 1962's "Lover Please" (pop #7, R&B #4) and "Little Bitty Pretty One" (pop #25) doing well. Unbeknownst to anyone at the time, "Little Bitty Pretty One" would be his last Top 40 hit on the pop charts. Thereafter, he recorded for several labels up through 1970, but there were no hits.

McPhatter's decline was linked largely to alcoholism, which resulted in him missing performances and exhibiting increasingly erratic behavior. He seemed to be unable to handle the drop-off in popularity that all but a select few performers find to be inevitable, but like many soul performers in the mid- to late 1960s, he discovered he had quite a following in England and moved there from 1966 to 1970. He wasn't content just as an oldies act, however, and he once made the claim that by the 1970s he had no fans, feeling they had let him down by abandoning him. Alcoholism, depression and poor health (he developed heart, kidney, liver disease) led to his death from a heart attack in 1972 when he was just thirty-nine years old.

3. "Idol with the Golden Head" | The Coasters (1957)

The Coasters had their origins in the 1940s in a variety of groups with ever-changing memberships, and as recounted in chapter 1, they first charted with "Down in Mexico," which kicked off a long string of sustained chart hits when it went to #8 on the R&B charts in 1956. "Young Blood" went to #8 in 1957 and #1 on the R&B chart, while its flip side, "Searchin,'" did even better by charting at #3 and also #1 on the R&B chart. Their third chart record in 1957 was "Idol with the Golden Head," a novelty-type song that was catchy enough for dancing and singing along. Another Leiber-Stoller composition, oddly enough it didn't make the R&B charts at all, though it did make the pop charts, stalling at #64.

The next year, the group charted with "Yakety Yak," followed by mainstays such as "Charlie Brown," "Along Came Jones" and "Poison Ivy," all of which peaked by August 1959. "Poison Ivy" was their last Top 10 hit, and in fact, on their next ten releases, only one made the Top 40 on the pop charts, "Little Egypt"(#23) in 1961. By the early 1960s, however, their doo-wop novelty songs had become somewhat passé, so after 1961, they charted only twice more.

4. "The Entertainer" | Tony Clarke (1964)

Tony Clarke was born in New York City as Ralph Thomas Williams, though some sources suggest that in fact his name may have been Ralph Ferguson or Ralph Clarke. He was raised in Detroit, and he was training to be a chef when he decided to pursue a career in music instead. He first recorded as Tall Tonio with the Mello-Dees for Stepp in 1960 and next on the Fascination label in 1962 under the name Tony Clarke. Neither effort was a hit.

While his career as a performer might have been lackluster, that certainly wasn't true of his career as a songwriter. In 1963, two of his songs charted for Etta James, "Pushover" (#25) and "Two Sides to Every Story" (#63). Clarke was also writing under his own name for other artists, such as the Vibrations and David Ruffin, and in addition he was writing under pseudonyms such as Tony Lois and even Thelma Williams.

Clarke was still trying to make it as a recording artist, and he signed with Chess and released two non-charting singles before his third, "The Entertainer," went big. With an organ-played introduction from "I Got Plenty O' Nothing" by way of George Gershwin's *Porgy and Bess*, the single rose to #31 on the *Billboard* Top 100 and went into the Top 10 on the R&B charts. The backup singers for "The Entertainer" were another Chess group, the Radiants, who that same year would have a hit with "Voice Your Choice" as well

as "Ain't No Big Thing." "The Entertainer" was backed with "This Heart of Mine," a good song that probably should have been a single release in its own right.

With the success of "The Entertainer," Tony Clarke went on tour with James Brown and even appeared on the Dick Clark Revue. Follow-up singles were not successful, however, although 1967's "Landslide" found an eager listening audience in England as a huge northern soul hit in the '70s, coming in at #15 of Kev Roberts's list of the Top 500 greatest northern soul hits of all time. Clarke moved to Hollywood, recorded some more and even appeared in the Sidney Poitier film *They Call Me Mr. Tibbs!*, where he had a bit part as a detective.

Considering that by 1970 he'd been in a movie, written for Etta James and David Ruffin and had his own hit single, it would seem that the world would be hearing a lot more about Tony Clarke in the coming years. Unfortunately, after he broke into his estranged wife's house during a domestic dispute, she shot him in the arm in self-defense, but the bullet ricocheted into his chest and killed him. He was thirty-one years old.

5. "Nip Sip" | The Clovers (1955)

The Clovers originated around 1946 in Washington, D.C., as the 4 Clovers, and eventually changed their name and signed with Atlantic records (for complete details, see chapter 1 on "One Mint Julep"). Their first two single releases, "Don't You Know I Love You" and "Fool, Fool, Fool," both went to #1 on the R&B charts, and their careers took off.

In December 1951, they recorded some new songs at Atlantic studios, among them the "drinking song" named "One Mint Julep," which was released in March 1952 and went to #2 on the R&B charts. Twelve Top 10 R&B hits later, they released another "drinking song," "Nip Sip." "Nip Sip" was written by songwriter Rudy Toombs, who had also written "One Mint Julep" as well as hits for Ruth Brown, Amos Milburn and Little

Willie John, among others. Although the song did not make the pop charts—not unusual for a song by Black artists at the time—it did go to #10 on the R&B charts. The flip side, "If I Could Be Loved by You," was another good beach song that has been anthologized.

After "Nip Sip" in 1955, the Clovers had three more Top 10 hits in 1956 but didn't hit it big again until 1959 with "Love Potion #9." It would be their last chart record, but with twenty-one chart records, many of them R&B and beach favorites, the Clovers remain one of the premier groups of the early years of beach music.

6. "I (Who Have Nothing)" | Ben E. King (1963)

Benjamin Earl Nelson moved to Harlem when he was nine years old. When he was eighteen, he was working at his father's restaurant when talent scout Lover Patterson heard him sing and asked if he could bring over four singers he was managing to see if they could gel as a group. They sounded good together, and Patterson signed King to join the Five Crowns. They eventually booked a performance at the Apollo in 1958, and Drifters' manager George Treadwell saw them perform. After Clyde McPhatter left the Drifters, Treadwell decided to fire the other group members and transform the Crowns into a new Drifters group to capitalize on the well-known name. Despite some early growing pains, by 1959, the group was recording new material, including a song King had written called "There Goes My Baby" (see chapter 1), which went to #2. The King-led group recorded a number of hits, including "Dance with Me," "This Magic Moment" and the #1 smash "Save the Last Dance for Me."

King (he changed his name around 1960) decided to go solo, and his second solo release was 1961's "Spanish Harlem," which went to #10 on the pop charts. King followed this up with 1961's "Stand by Me," written by King and Leiber and Stoller and inspired by a spiritual written by Sam Cooke. It was King's biggest hit, peaking at #1 on the R&B charts, #4 on the pop charts and then going to #9 again in 1986 when the movie *Stand By Me* was released; it hit #1 in England in 1987. King went on to have a number of chart hits in the ensuing years, such as "Amor" (#18 pop, 1961), "Don't Play That Song"(#11 pop, 1962), "I (Who Have Nothing)"(#29 pop, 1963). "I (Who Have Nothing)" was actually a cover version of an Italian song "Uno dei Tanti" with English lyrics by Leiber and Stoller, and it reached #29 on the pop charts and #16 on the R&B charts. This song may in fact be the oddest selection on the album, given that there were better King songs and this song would not endure as a popular beach song, probably due to its slow pacing.

King passed away in 2015.

3

THE ALBUM THAT WASN'T REALLY A *BEACH* MUSIC ALBUM: *SUMMER SOUVENIRS*

BELL 6035, 1969

*A*fter the release of the two Atlantic *Beach Beat* albums, if you walked into a record store and saw *Summer Souvenirs* marketed as a beach music album, you might have believed it if you just glanced at the front sleeve. James and Bobby Purify, Clifford Curry, Maurice Williams and the Zodiacs and Don Gardner and Dee Dee Ford all had songs that were reputable beach music selections. The Five Satins, the Silhouettes and Buster Brown were not really beach music, but old-style '50s doo-wop and R&B is pretty close—so maybe. The real tip-off on the sleeve should have been Ronny & the Daytonas—that's a hard no. So was it supposed to be a beach music album or not? Ed Weiss told me it was, and despite what it said on the sleeve, he had nothing to do with it.

"The Atlantic albums did well enough that Larry Uttal, president at Bell Records, decided to put out an album called *Summer Souvenirs*," Weiss told me. "It wasn't all beach music because it had 'GTO ' by Ronny & the Daytonas and 'Little Girl' by the Syndicate of Sound, but I think he got the idea from what we had done with Atlantic. It had Clifford Curry 'She Shot a Hole' and 'We're Gonna Hate Ourselves,' and some others that *were* beach music. It was not really a beach music album, but it was born out of the two Atlantic LPs."

By the late 1960s, Bell Records had ties to nearly sixty subsidiary and acquired labels, which may be why the choices on the album are all over the place. The songs by Clifford Curry, James and Bobby Purify, Maurice Williams and Don Gardner and Dee Dee Ford are undisputed beach classics, and the selections by Bob Kuban and Buster Brown are passable. But doo-wop tracks by the Silhouettes and the Five Satins make no sense, and the Lee Dorsey track is standard R&B. Worse yet, "G.T.O." and "Little Girl" are rock/pop tracks that were less than five years old. This album clearly drew some good beach tunes from the available catalogue and then filled the gaps with songs Bell owned the rights to. But if they *really* wanted a beach music album, what could have been here? Bell and its subsidiary labels had the rights to "I Dig Your Act" by the O'Jays, a (now) classic time-tested beach song. Bell also had the right to some good James and Bobby Purify tracks in addition to "I'm Your Puppet," including "Wish You Didn't Have to Go" and "Let Love Come Between Us." Finally, the Van Dykes' "You're Shakin' Me Up" had been released on Bell's subsidiary Mala label in 1966, and it was a good second-level beach song. Take off a few of the weaker non-beach tunes here, add these four and you have a pretty solid album.

Perhaps it may have been they were trying to appeal to buyers on both coasts or oldie enthusiasts or both, and hence some of the odder, non–beach music choices. Or maybe Bell didn't have anyone to advise them who really knew beach music, because it's hard to speculate on why you'd pass on good songs you had the rights to, but they did just that. And make no mistake, though Weiss and the KIX Men of Music were acknowledged on the album, Weiss says they were not involved. The liner notes thank the "KIX Music Men—Radio Station WKIX, Raleigh North Carolina," including Charlie Brown, by name, but "I didn't have really thing to do with it, though he gave the KIX Men of Music credit on the back of album," Weiss said. It may have been that giving a shout-out to the KIX Men of Music was only an effort to market the album and maybe pick up some credibility along the way. After all, they'd been acknowledged on the second Atlantic album, and Weiss had also been mentioned on the back cover of the first Atlantic album, so the mention may have been to tie it into the Atlantic beach music albums.

Weiss said he didn't think the album sold well, which is not surprising since there was a lack of identity. The Atlantic albums were built around songs that weren't available anymore, and many of them had been released more than a decade earlier. Most of the true beach music cuts on *Summer Souvenirs*, such as the Clifford Curry and James and Bobby Purify tracks, were just two years old. The principal tracks that might be "hard to find" in 1969—more than a decade old—were the Silhouettes, Five Satins and Buster Brown tracks, and no true beach music enthusiast was likely to buy an album just to get those.

One thing is for sure, and that is that after this album there wouldn't be another beach music compilation album for almost ten years. Perhaps declining sales for each album and the feeling that the experiment had been tried and had failed was the cause, but certainly this weak album didn't help things.

SUMMER SOUVENIRS (BELL 6035, 1969)

Side 1
1. Clifford Curry, "She Shot a Hole in My Soul"
2. The Five Satins, "To the Aisle"
3. Lee Dorsey, "Ride Your Pony"
4. The Syndicate of Sound, "Little Girl"
5. James and Bobby Purify, "I'm Your Puppet"
6. The Silhouettes, "Get a Job"
7. Maurice Williams and the Zodiacs, "Stay"

Side 2
1. Don Gardner and Dee Dee Ford, "I Need Your Lovin'"
2. Ronny & the Daytonas, "G.T.O."
3. Clifford Curry, "We're Gonna Hate Ourselves in the Morning"
4. Bob Kuban, "The Cheater "
5. Buster Brown, "Fannie Mae"
6. The Five Satins, "In the Still of the Night (I'll Remember)"

The Songs

Sometimes there's a fine line between what one person thinks is a beach song and what another person thinks is a beach song. However, no beach music fan would argue that "To the Aisle," "Ride Your Pony," "Little Girl," "Get a Job," "G.T.O." and "In The Still of The Night" are beach music. Consequently, there are only brief entries for these songs.

Side 1

1. "She Shot a Hole in My Soul" | Clifford Curry (1967)

Clifford Curry started his musical career as a member of the doowop group the Five Pennies, but by 1959, Curry had decided to go back home to Tennessee to pursue a solo career. He recorded a few singles for Excello, and when Curry was touring, he met producer Buzz Cason, who liked Curry's voice and decided to give him the chance to record a couple of songs.

First Curry recorded "She Shot a Hole in My Soul," and he told me, "We felt really good about it, and we believed it was going to chart." Their intuition was correct, and after being released on Elf records, the song reached #95 on the Hot 100 and #45 on the R&B charts.

To his surprise, Curry suddenly discovered he was in big demand in the Carolinas. "I had no idea the songs were going to fit into the beach music thing like they did," he told me.

> *I was just a singer trying to have a hit. Robert Hunicutt had a club in North Carolina called Williams Lake, [and] that was my first gig [in] the Carolinas. I played that week, and he had a friend in Myrtle Beach named Cecil Corbett who had the Beach Club. He hired me the next weekend, Easter weekend, when the kids were out on school break. Those two weeks were the best two weeks I ever had in my career. That's what got me into beach music.*

Curry didn't follow up with any recordings as big as "She Shot a Hole in My Soul" and admitted, "I had a career lull after 'She Shot a Hole.' Buzz just wasn't familiar with the whole beach music thing, and we were doing things that just weren't being recognized in the Carolinas. It wasn't beach music." Curry later recorded for several labels, but since none were targeted toward beach music audiences, his songs didn't seem to be catching on.

Curry's story is continued on side 2 in the write-up for "We're Gonna Hate Ourselves in the Morning."

2. "To the Aisle" | The Five Satins (1957)

"To the Aisle" by the Five Satins is a classic R&B song, but it's slow and definitely not a beach song. It was an extremely odd choice, and one can only speculate that given that Bell had the rights and it had been a proven Top 40 hit more than a decade earlier, they must have included it for the name recognition.

3. "Ride Your Pony" | Lee Dorsey (1965)

Lee Dorsey recorded a number of solid R&B hits in the 1960s, including "Ya Ya," which went to #7 on the *Billboard* Hot 100 and #1 on the R&B charts in 1961. "Ride Your Pony" went to #7 on the R&B, while "Working in the Coal Mine" peaked at #5. His songs are not typically considered beach music, however.

4. "Little Girl" | The Syndicate of Sound (1966)

While "Little Girl" is definitely a classic and one of the finest garage rock songs ever recorded, it isn't a beach song or even a summer song. It was another odd choice for this album thematically. The song had peaked at #8 on the *Billboard* pop charts.

5. "I'm Your Puppet" | James and Bobby Purify (1966)

In 1963, Robert Lee Dickey dropped by a Florida nightclub to see a performance by his cousin James Purify's group, the Dothan Sextet. The group's guitarist had quit that night, and Dickey joined them on stage to get them through their set. They asked him to join the group on a permanent basis, and by 1965, they were touring with and backing up the likes of Otis Redding, Wilson Pickett and James Brown. In 1966, producer "Papa Don" Schroeder heard the group and offered Purify and Dickey recording contracts.

Schroder gave them a song called "I'm Your Puppet," written by Muscle Shoals mainstays Dan Penn and Spooner Oldham. Schroeder felt it would be a good song for Dickey, but he told Bill Dahl, "I don't think either one of them liked the song, because it wasn't R&B enough to suit [them]." Furthermore, Dickey couldn't sing the song correctly, but when Purify took lead, everything clicked. Still, it was a grueling recording session, and Schroeder noted that "it was a twenty-something-hour session, 'cause we were cutting mono. You had to get it all in one time. Then you've got to come back and do your overdubs." In a 2000 interview with the *Florida Democrat*, Dickey said of the song, "I hated it. It was originally intended to be the B-side. But things got changed....I sang it for 23 hours straight (in the studio), that's why I hate it. And the last one, the last take was the one they decided to go with." They were rechristened James and Bobby Purify to market the song and released "I'm Your Puppet" in September 1966. It peaked at #5 on the R&B charts and #6 on the pop charts.

Although their debut chart single would be their highest charting record, they continued to release some quality sides. Their second single, "Wish You Didn't Have to Go," was a moderate hit, as was a cover of the Five Du-Tones raucous hit "Shake a Tail Feather." Another cover, "Let Love Come Between Us," released in 1967, would be their second-biggest hit and went to #23 on the pop charts. Schroder said he had achieved his goal of cutting "a real good beach hit. It's one of my favorite records that I cut on the Purifys."

It would be James and Bobby Purify's last Top 40 hit. The group went on to record some moderately successful songs after that, but Dickey quit by 1972. Purify brought in Ben Moore to sing as Bobby Purify, but the magic was gone. Dickey passed away in 2012.

6. "Get a Job" | The Silhouettes (1958)

When "Get a Job" was released nationally, it sold more than one million copies in just three weeks and reached #1 on both the *Billboard* pop and R&B charts by February 1958. Like the Five Satins' "In the Still of the Night," this is a fine song and a doo-wop classic, but it was clearly not a beach music selection.

7. "Stay" | Maurice Williams and the Zodiacs (1960)

As was recounted in chapter 2, by the early 1950s, Maurice Williams had formed a group and was writing songs. They recorded a song he'd written called "Little Darlin'," and when released on the Excello label in 1957, it reached #41 on the pop charts and #11 on the R&B charts.

After a few more singles, they left Excello, and after hearing about a car called a Zodiac made in the 1950s for the European market, they adopted the name. They recorded a couple of singles on small labels before signing with Herald Records in 1960, where they recorded another song by Williams called "Stay." He'd written the song years earlier about a girl and the night she had to leave because she had to be home by 10:00 p.m. He apparently didn't think as much of the song as he did the girl, however, and he told Marion Carter, "I had never thought too much about 'Stay' and had thrown the lyrics in the trash. However, I still had a demo tape and one night we were playing demos and my girlfriend's sister heard it and went crazy over it. That changed my thinking, and we used the song as a demo for Herald

Records." Williams did change the original lyrics, however, and a line that referred to smoking cigarettes was changed because it was likely to offend parents. Herald released "Stay," and audiences loved hearing about Williams's efforts to persuade his girlfriend to remain past her curfew as he assures her that her parents won't mind if she stays for just one more dance—not one more smoke. By November, the record had reached #1, and at one minute and thirty-seven seconds, the record is well known for being at the shortest #1 record in the history of the *Billboard* pop charts. It is estimated that the record has sold more than ten million copies.

Maurice Williams and the Zodiacs were far from done, however: "I Remember" is discussed in chapter 4 (*Billy Smith's Beach Party Volume 2*) and "May I" and the group's later career are covered in chapter 2 (*Beach Beat Vol. 2*). The group continued to release occasional singles on different labels right up into the 1980s.

Side 2
1. "I Need Your Lovin'" | Don Gardner and Dee Dee Ford (1962)

Donald Gardner got his start as a drummer in the late 1940s before he got his chance to record a few sides as a vocalist. By the late '50s, he was recording simply as Don Gardner for a variety of labels, but none of those efforts were successful on the charts.

By the early 1960s, Wrecia Holloway (whose real name was actually Wrecia Mae Ford) was performing with Gardner. A talented keyboardist with a strong background in gospel, Holloway, who went by the stage name Dee Dee Ford, brought a different sound to Gardner's act, as he became more firmly entrenched in and served the R&B market. Gardner and his band were seen performing by another artist, Arthur "Big Boy" Crudup. Crudup recorded for Bobby Robinson, owner of the Fire and Fury record labels, who counted among its artists Buster Brown, Wilbert Harrison and the pre-Motown Gladys Knight and the Pips. Crudup convinced Robinson to catch Gardner and Ford's act, and Robinson saw them perform a screamer of a number Gardner had written called "I Need Your Lovin'." He signed them to the Fire label.

When performed live, "I Need Your Lovin'" ran as long as five or six minutes, with a long, soulful buildup, which was really a very different song from the second part (often done as an encore), which kicked in right after Gardner hit "Wo-wo-wo-

wo-wo-wo-wo!" nearly three minutes into the song. Though Fire had the group record a long version, they cut off the last two minutes and forty-three seconds and issued that part of the song as a single in 1962. It reached #20 on the *Billboard* pop charts and broke into the Top 10 on the R&B charts. Their next side for Fire, "Don't You Worry," also went to the Top 10 on the R&B charts, but after one more single for Fire, they left the label. Gardner and Ford recorded for several other small labels before they broke up their act by 1965. Ford (now as Wrecia Holloway) focused on writing songs and wrote "Let Me Down Easy" for Betty (later Bettye) LaVette, which made the Top 20 on the R&B charts. Gardner continued to record, but other than a 1973 duet with Baby Washington, "Forever," nothing charted. As of this writing, Gardner is still living; Ford left the music business and died in 1972.

2. "G.T.O." | Ronny & The Daytonas (1964)

This song came out in the 1960s when music about fast cars were the rage, and it went to #4 on the national pop charts and sold one million records. It is obviously not *Carolina* beach music, but Bell records tried to shoehorn this hit from subsidiary label Mala into this album nevertheless.

3. "We're Gonna Hate Ourselves in the Morning" | Clifford Curry (1967)

When listeners flipped over the single "She Shot a Hole in My Soul," they were delighted to find a song every bit as good—some might say better—on the B side. The song was a tune the great Arthur Alexander had co-

written called "We're Gonna Hate Ourselves in the Morning," a song producer Buzz Cason and even Curry thought was just a filler. "We didn't have any idea it was going to be a hit," Curry said. "We had the horn arrangements written out for the horn players to play, and Buzz decided not to use them. He figured it was just a B side so he sent the horn players home to save some money." It didn't chart nationally, but in the Carolinas, it was big, and airplay there got both songs noticed. Consequently, on the beach music scene, Curry had not one but two big hits, so the popularity he found in the Carolinas should have come as no surprise.

After several more releases but no further hits at Elf, Curry recorded for several small labels, but said since none of his output was targeted toward beach music audiences, his songs didn't seem to be catching on. His roots in beach music resurfaced in 1980 when he released "Shag with Me," and although the record didn't chart nationally, it appears on the third Ripete *Beach Beat* album. Though Curry would never again have a national hit record, he remained a major figure on the Carolina beach music circuit until his death in 2016.

4. "The Cheater" | Bob Kuban and the In-Men (1965)

As odd as it may seem, the fast-paced beat of "The Cheater" didn't mean it wasn't accepted as a beach song, and in fact, it's usually seen as one of those fast-shagging/collegiate bop–type tunes. It wasn't a popular R&B/beach mainstay, but it did make some beach music playlists.

Bob Kuban graduated from Washington University and the St. Louis Institute of Music and in 1963 started teaching music. In 1964, he had a band called the Rhythm Masters when he met a lead vocalist Walter Notheis, a.k.a. "Sir" Walter Scott, who was singing with the Pacemakers. Notheis joined Kuban's band, and as the Bob Kuban Band they cut a couple of songs that were regionally popular. It wasn't until 1965 as the newly christened Bob Kuban and the In-Men that Kuban and his bandmates established themselves as a feature act. One band member had written a song called "The Cheater," which was recorded in St. Louis on the Musicland label. Originally, the song was written in the first person ("Look out for me, I'm a Cheater"), but Kuban said, "I wanted to do a song that had excitement to it, had some energy and had a good driving tempo, so we added a bridge and put it in the third person." These alterations made the song

a winner, and the record peaked at #12 on the *Billboard* charts and earned a gold record. The group appeared on television on programs such as *Where the Action Is* and *American Bandstand*, and the song went all the way to #1 in Australia.

With the success of "The Cheater," they headed back to the studio and recorded a follow-up, "The Teaser." Kuban said, "I hated the song, and even today I have never played it live. I fought with our manager about releasing it after 'The Cheater' because I knew a hit record needed a strong follow-up, and 'The Teaser' wasn't it." Surprisingly, "The Teaser" actually did chart (#70), followed by a cover of the Beatles' "Drive My Car" (#93). Three chart records in a row did seem to promise great things ahead for the band.

Unfortunately, Notheis was soon lured away from the band for a solo career, and after he left and some other membership changes, the group really never gelled again. Despite the acrimony of the group's split, nearly twenty years after their dissolution, the band was preparing for a big reunion concert when Walter Scott was murdered in December 1983. Kuban continues to perform to this day, and the other members of the band have gone on to be successful in their fields as well.

5. "Fannie Mae"| Buster Brown (1959)

Some details of Buster Brown's early life are confusing outside of the fact that he was born in Georgia. His name may actually have been "Buster" Brown, and while some older reference works say that he was born Waymon Glasco, more up-to-date sources now refute this. What is certain is that for more than forty years, Brown remained in Georgia, and he apparently did play part-time gigs in the 1930s and '40s. Then, as later, he was known for playing the harmonica. In the 1950s, he decided to make the move to New York and pursue a career as a professional entertainer. He auditioned for Bobby Robinson, who owned the Fire and Fury record labels. In 1959, Robinson had just released Wilbert Harrison's #1 record "Kansas City" on Fury, and while looking for the label's next big hit, he had Brown come in for an audition. Brown sang an a cappella version of a song he had written himself called "Fannie Mae." Robinson liked what he heard and quickly assembled some of his regular studio musicians. After just two takes, they had a recording that Robinson felt was good enough to release, and indeed it did eventually go to #1 on the R&B charts. Brian Wilson later stated that the song was influential for the Beach Boys, in particular, "Help Me Rhonda."

Brown released an album on Fire in 1961, but other than two low-charting singles, further chart success eluded him. Brown left Fire shortly thereafter, and a series of singles during the 1960s on small labels brought no further success. Brown passed away in Brooklyn in 1976.

6. "In the Still of the Night (I'll Remember)" | The Five Satins (1956)

This million-seller is generally considered one of the most important records in rock-and-roll history. The second Five Satins selection on this album, the song hit #24 on the pop charts and #3 on the R&B charts. It is not generally considered a beach song, however.

4

NO RIGHTS? NO PERMISSIONS? NO PROBLEM! THE BILLY SMITH BOOTLEGS

*U*p until this point, the three albums targeting beach music audiences had been pretty consistent. On *Beach Beat*, Atlantic Records included high-demand songs, but only ones they had the rights to on their Atlantic label and their Atco subsidiary. On *Beach Beat Volume 2*, the Atlantic and Atco recordings were supplemented by acquiring licensing for some of the titles held by Chess Records and Dee-Su. The third beach music compilation album, *Summer Souvenirs*, also used songs that the parent company, Bell Records, had the rights to, as well as tracks from labels with which Bell had distribution deals.

Even with such a broad reach, after the first three albums, undoubtedly many people wondered about the untapped potential of songs on Minit, Imperial, ABC-Paramount, Smash, Federal and many other labels. And in terms of beach music, these weren't obscure titles that would force the producers of the albums to use substandard fillers (as Bell Records had). In this case, classics such as "39-21-40 Shape," "Sixty Minute Man," "Double Shot," "With This Ring," "Anna," "I Got the Fever" and many others were still uncollected. No doubt just the process of acquiring the rights and the masters from such a variety of labels (some of which were no longer in business) would have been a nightmare, not to mention the costs that might have been incurred. Perhaps this left anyone considering a similar project with the sense that a more complicated and perhaps more expensive undertaking wasn't worth the trouble. Consequently, there were no more beach music compilation albums for roughly a decade after *Summer Souvenirs,* and while that certainly didn't mean there was no demand, it seemed no one was willing to invest in such a big project that may or may not bring in a profit.

But during the early 1970s, beach music started growing and expanding to include newer material and more regional material as well. The result was that it was becoming more and more popular, and not just at the beach, but on college campuses across the South. Although there had been no new compilation albums, the popularity and availability of the 8-track tape player and recorder from the late 1960s on meant that almost anyone could make compilation tapes, and it seemed like everyone did. It's one thing to do it for personal use, but mass producing them for sale without acquiring the rights (called "pirating" or "bootlegging") became a huge black market industry. The first beach music compilation tape I ever bought was in a shop selling bootleg 8-tracks about a block from the Myrtle Beach Pavilion. Anyone who saw them knew they weren't original releases because they were cheap, had generic pictures on them, often had misspellings on the labels and frankly they didn't sound all that great. But for a college student on a budget, they were a bargain. That first tape I bought—simply called *Beach Music Hits*—contained tracks previously unavailable on a compilation by artists such as Brenton Wood, Jewell and the Rubies, Arthur Alexander, the Georgia Prophets, the Monzas and many others. In fact, none of the songs on that tape I bought had appeared on a compilation album, so even in the mid-1970s some of the best beach music produced over the previous three decades was still unavailable on compilation albums or tapes. There was clearly a void to be filled on vinyl too, and someone needed to step into the breach. That person, as it turned out, was Billy Smith, a DJ at WNMB in North Myrtle Beach.

William M. "Billy" Smith was born in Marion, South Carolina, and grew up with a love for rhythm and blues music, music he often heard

Billy Smith's Beach Party

10 great beach classics

FOR DANCERS

RAINY DAY BELLS
Globetrotters

LAUGH IT OFF
The Tams

ACROSS THE STREET
Lenny O Henry

MISS GRACE
Tymes

INVENTORY ON HEARTACHES
Bob Collins

FOR LOVERS

SO MUCH IN LOVE
Tymes

39 21 40 SHAPE
Showmen

GOTTA HAVE YOUR LOVE
Blue Swede

LONELY DRIFTER
O' Jays

WONDERFUL SUMMER
Robin Ward

Billy Smith's Beach Party

Engineered by Bill Norman
Produced by Deane Morris

Special Thanks to Linda, Tommy, Cindy
Don Reid and all the people that
love "BEACH CLASSICS"

playing on the boardwalk or at the Pavilion when he and his family would go to Myrtle Beach after church on Sundays. He got his first job on Marion's WATP AM, the first in a series of jobs that would later include WTGR in Myrtle Beach and WNMB in North Myrtle Beach. He became one of the most popular on-air personalities in the Carolinas, and he went on to win numerous awards, such as "Beach Music DJ of the Year." He was also inducted into the Beach Music Hall of Fame in 2001. Simply put, if you loved beach music back in the '70s and '80s, you listened to Billy Smith. As Chris Beachley, a mover and shaker in the beach music industry, told me, Smith was "really instrumental [in the development] of beach music in Myrtle Beach."

In 1978, Billy Smith went to his friend, Myrtle Beach entrepreneur Deane Morris with a business proposal—he wanted to create a new beach music compilation album. Morris told me, "I knew Billy pretty well, and he told me he had an album he wanted to produce but he didn't have the money. He said it would take $1,000, and we'd get one thousand albums." Morris agreed to front Smith the money, and through his connections, Smith used the money and had the albums pressed. Morris was surprised, however, "when the album came out in 1979 and my name was on it as producer. I thought it was kind of him to do that." Morris said, "My brother had a radio station in Savannah, and we put it on the air down there," and of course Smith was also frequently mentioning the album on WNMB. Morris was also "an investor in the Dutch Deli," and as a result, they were also "selling [the albums] at the Dutch Deli and wherever we could." Sales were good, and the albums were doing well. But then things went off the rails.

Morris recalled an encounter at work one day:

This guy comes in and says, "Are you Deane Morris?" And I said, "Yeah."
He said, "I'd like to talk with you." I said, "Just have a seat," and he

said, "No, I'd like to talk to you in private. First why don't we go into your office, and if you want to come back out here talk after that I'll be glad to." So I go in my office and close the door and he flashes his FBI badge and says, "You know anything about this Billy Smith's Beach Party *album?" I said I did and he said, "You know, you have to get copyrights for all those songs when you reproduce them." I said, "I had nothing to do with that album except to lend him the money!" He said, "Well it says produced by Deane Morris right here."*

It seems that Billy Smith hadn't acquired the rights for the songs—which would explain why none of the usual songwriting and label credits were on the album cover or the record label. "Since I didn't *really* produce the album, I didn't have to know anything about copyright, and Billy probably knew about it but thought he could get away with it," Morris told me. "Frankly, I think he was surprised any of the beach music artists would have come after him. But the guys who put the law on him were the Globetrotters." "Rainy Day Bells" was recorded on the Kirshner label, and it shouldn't have been surprising that the label would come after him. At the time, Don Kirshner was one of the biggest names in the music business, and it wouldn't do to send the message that a Kirshner product could be pirated without consequences.

Smith and Morris were facing copyright violation charges, but at first it looked like they would get off easy. "We were told that the process would be simple," Morris said.

We'd go before a judge, plead no contest, sign off on it, pay a fine and be done. Well, we're at the federal courthouse in Charleston, and the judge says, "Do y'all realize what you're doing? You're pleading guilty to the pirating of copyrights and that could have a fine and a five-year probation and jail time." And I said, "Whoa! Whoa! Whoa! I don't even have a lawyer. We didn't know anything about this." He said, "Why don't you let me finish?"—It scared the shit out of me. He said, "You're going to be on probation for one year." I said, "Probation? That's not what we were told." He said, "Well you can go back and get a lawyer and fight this, but you will not win, Mr. Morris, because you did produce the record." Now, you've got to remember Billy Smith was a loose cannon anyway, and the whole time Billy was mocking the judge and I'm saying, "Shut up Billy, shut up!" For the next year, I couldn't even go out of town without calling this guy. I felt like a damn criminal.

Today Morris looks back on it as a learning experience. "I can kinda laugh about it now," he said. "But I wasn't laughing then." They paid their fines and went on probation, and of course they had to quit selling the albums. But lucky buyers who had picked up one of these rarities were in a for a treat—probably the best compilation album up until that time.

BILLY SMITH'S BEACH PARTY: 10 GREAT BEACH CLASSICS
(NO RECORD COMPANY LISTED, 904027-2902)

Titles and groups are listed as they appear on the jacket.

FOR DANCERS
Rainy Day Bells, Globetrotters
Laugh It Off, The Tams
Across The Street, Lenny O Henry
Miss Grace, Tymes
Inventory on Heartaches, Bob Collins

FOR LOVERS
So Much in Love, Tymes
39 21 40 Shape, Showmen
Gotta Have Your Love, Blue Swede
Lonely Drifter, O' Jays
Wonderful Summer, Robin Ward

THE TRACK LISTINGS ABOVE are taken directly from the album with song titles and group credits exactly as they appear on the album. Obviously, there are several misspellings and grammatical issues on the track listings, and the sleeve looks amateurish in a way that harkens back to those bootleg 8-tracks on Ocean Boulevard. A generic stock picture on the front (again, à la those bootleg 8-tracks) and the lack of almost any liner notes or a record label name reinforce that idea. This is not to nitpick but to show it was rather carelessly put together.

Still, there are many positives as well, and other than "Across the Street," none of these songs had been on previous compilation albums. Only two of the selected tracks seem odd choices today: the beach-themed but not-really-beach-music selection "Wonderful Summer" by Robin Ward and the forgettable "Gotta Have Your Love" by Blue Swede. Since "Wonderful Summer" was the last song on the album, perhaps its title and the sounds of waves crashing made it a fitting finale for the album (it's worth noting that both "So Much in Love" and "Lonely Drifter" on the "For Lovers" side also have the sounds of surf and seagulls). It's really hard to justify the inclusion of Blue Swede under any circumstances, however. Morris said "Billy had picked all the music from songs that were pretty hot at the time," but that's all he knew about Smith's methodology for selecting tracks. Certainly few (if any) people would include "Gotta Have Your Love" on any beach music playlist today.

The minimal liner notes said, "Special Thanks to Linda, Tommy, Cindy, Don Reid and all the people that love 'BEACH CLASSICS.' Hear Billy Smith's Beach Party Saturdays from 2 until 7 on WNMB STEREO 105." It also read, "Engineered by Bill Norman" and finally the words that caused a lot of trouble for his investor, "Produced by Deane Morris."

The Songs

Side I: FOR DANCERS
1. "Rainy Day Bells" | The Globetrotters (1970)

In 1970, Hanna-Barbera developed a Saturday morning cartoon based on the touring basketball team the Harlem Globetrotters. From 1970 to 1972, twenty-two episodes featuring characters based on real Globetrotters such as "Meadowlark" Lemon were produced, and much like the "gang" in Hanna-Barbera staples such as *Scooby Doo, Where Are You?* and *Josie and the Pussy Cats*, the team members often find themselves up against evildoers but reign supreme in the end. Like other cartoons at the time, the main characters would often sing and perform so that Hanna-Barbera could

cash in on the cartoon's popularity by having the characters release an album and a few singles.

Hanna-Barbera brought in producer Jeff Barry and involved series music supervisor Don Kirshner. One of the songs recorded was the Neil Sedaka and Howie Greenfield tune "Rainy Day Bells." "When we recorded 'Rainy Day Bells' I thought it was a nice, catchy little tune, but that's it. I didn't think it would be popular," Meadowlark Lemon told me in an interview. "Rainy Day Bells" was indeed a good song, and it was rumored that it was the team themselves singing it. That was partially true, and Lemon said, "I did sing background, but they had some great professional studio singers and musicians there to put that thing together, and they, not the team, sang it." Other singers at the session were vocalists such as Sammy Turner (who had charted with "Lavender Blue" in 1959), J.R. Bailey (formerly of the Cadillacs), Robert Spencer (also of the Cadillacs and Crazy Elephant) and Rudy Clark (singer and also writer of such hits as "The Shoop-Shoop Song"). The song had a late '50s/early '60s doo-wop sound, and when released as a single, it was not a big seller.

For beach music fans, the song was one of the most desirable and hard-to-find singles in the 1970s. It hadn't had a wide distribution and didn't chart, and how many people were likely to buy a single or an album by cartoon characters when it wasn't a hit? Copies of the 45 were scarce and expensive, and its inclusion on the Billy Smith LP would have sold a whole lot of these albums.

2. "Laugh It Off" | The Tams (1963)

Nothing spotlights the problem facing the unavailability of beach music classics better than the story of the Tams, who are considered beach music royalty today. They had six records in the *Billboard* Pop Top 100 (one Top Ten), seven songs in the R&B charts Top 100 and even two Top 40 songs on the British charts, including "Hey Girl, Don't Bother Me," which hit #1. Nevertheless, they had not been included on any of the previous compilation albums, no doubt due to licensing issues and what it might cost to get the rights from ABC-Paramount. But even in 1979, they were still playing to packed houses across the South as one of the most highly regarded beach music acts of all time.

The Tams originated in Atlanta, Georgia, and started as the Four Dots. Led by brothers Joe Pope and Charles Pope, they played in Atlanta-area clubs in the 1950s, wearing blue tam-o'-shanter hats because, as Charles

Pope told me, "We really couldn't afford anything else." Taking their cue from their stage wear, they became the Tams. They eventually came to the attention of Atlanta song publisher and entrepreneur Bill Lowery, who arranged for the group to record a song called "Untie Me," written by a then-unknown young writer and musician named Joe South. "Untie Me" climbed to #62 on the Hot 100 and #12 on the R&B charts.

The group started working with a young songwriter named Ray Whitley. Whitley was just twenty years old and would go on to write for Tommy Roe, Brian Hyland, the Swingin' Medallions and others. The first song he wrote for the Tams was called "What Kind of Fool (Do You Think I Am?)," and Larkin noted that ABC-Paramount picked up the song and it went #9 on the *Billboard* pop charts and #1 on the *Cash Box* R&B chart, even though, surprisingly, Charles Pope says that he "was surprised by 'What Kind of Fool,'" because he didn't like it much and "didn't even want that song to be our second release." Nevertheless, the combination of Whitley's songwriting and the Tams' voices seemed to be a recipe for success. The song was recorded at Rick Hall's FAME Studios in Muscle Shoals, Alabama, as was the song on the flip side, another Whitley composition called "Laugh It Off," which went on to become a beach music classic as well.

After this, the Tams had a long series of national and regional hits such as "Hey Girl, Don't Bother Me," "Be Young, Be Foolish, Be Happy" and many others. Despite having had hits for close to two decades, until the *Billy Smith's Beach Party* album, their music had not been on a beach music compilation record.

3. "Across the Street" | Lenny O'Henry

This is the first repeated track from the first three albums, having appeared on Atlantic's *Beach Beat Vol. 2*. See that album for details about the song.

4. "Ms. Grace" | The Tymes (1974)

The Philadelphia group started out as the Latineers, "because we thought the name sounded good, like we had a Latin sound," member Norm Burnett told me. After winning a radio station contest, they signed with Cameo-Parkway, which changed their name to the Tymes (for details on the early group, see the entry on "So Much in Love" on side 2 of this album). "So Much in Love" hit #1 on the pop charts and was followed by "Wonderful! Wonderful!" (#7), but after a few poorly performing records through 1964, they left Parkway. At this point, they were singing backup for other artists, even providing the background vocals for old labelmate Len Barry on his #2 smash "1-2-3." They signed with MGM, which dropped them after two non-charting releases, before they signed with Columbia. At Columbia, they had just one Top 40 hit, and by 1971, they were without a label once again.

Still searching for a label, the group's producer, Billy Jackson, had them cut some demos he hoped Kenny Gamble and Leon Huff would find suitable for their fledgling Philadelphia International label, but they passed and Jackson took the tapes to RCA. RCA signed the group and took the very song Gamble and Huff had passed on, "You Little Trustmaker," and released it in 1974. The song shot up to #12 on the *Billboard* pop charts, and the group was suddenly hot once again. They followed that with the release of what many people consider the greatest all-time beach music classic, 1974's "Ms. Grace." "Ms. Grace" was written by John and Johanna Hall (John became a member of the group Orleans, which would later chart with hits such as "Still the One"), and despite the chart impetus provided by the success of "You Little Trustmaker," "Ms. Grace" reached only #91 on the *Billboard* charts in the United States. In England, however, it soared all the way to #1. "It's a nice song, a different type of song," Norm Burnett told me, "a really beautiful song." Yet surprisingly, the Tymes' newfound success was short-lived, and after charting once more in 1976, there were no more chart records.

5. "Inventory on Heartaches" | Bob Collins and the Fabulous Five (1967)

North Carolina native Donny Trexler started performing before he was ten years old, and in 1959, "Chuck Tilley and I started a band known as the Six Teens," Trexler told me. They added nineteen-year-old Bob Collins to play drums, and when he turned twenty, "the 'Six Teens' name was no longer accurate and we changed the name to 'Chuck Tilley and the Fabulous Five.' Chuck was the lead singer, I was the guitar player and Bob played drums," Trexler said. Eventually, Tilley left, and when Collins moved up front in 1962, the group's new name became Bob Collins and the Fabulous Five.

In 1964, the group heard a song called "If I Didn't Have a Dime" by the Los Angeles–based Furys, a cover of a song that had appeared as the flip side of Gene Pitney's 1962 smash "Only Love Can Break a Heart." The group decided to incorporate the song into their act and even recorded it late in the summer of 1966. Although the single sold only regionally, the song's popularity contributed to the group's renown and led to them playing with the Four Tops, Martha and the Vandellas, Major Lance and many other acts. The Fabulous Five's next release was a song Trexler had written called "Inventory on Heartaches." They recorded it with Collins on lead and Trexler playing guitar and singing backup; Trexler arranged the song as well. Like many regionally recorded songs, "Inventory on Heartaches" didn't make an impression on the national charts and owes its subsequent success to its popularity on not only the beach music circuit but also the northern soul scene.

Oddly enough, by the time the single was released, Trexler was no longer with the group. He realized the group wasn't taking advantage of their opportunities or thinking big enough, and "I decided it was time to move on." Because the group had gotten some money up front from Mainline Records to record "Inventory on Heartaches," they released it even though Trexler told me he had by then joined Ted Carrol and the Music Era. Bob Collins and the Fabulous Five disbanded not long after Trexler left the group, while Trexler joined the O'Kaysions, then a band called Swing from 1972 until 1986 before ultimately performing with his wife, Susan. Trexler, who still owns the rights to the name Bob Collins and the Fabulous Five and their recordings, was inducted into the South Carolina Rhythm and Blues Hall of Fame, among other accolades.

Side 2: FOR LOVERS
1. "So Much in Love" | The Tymes (1963)

Considering that Smith wasn't paying royalties anyway, it's odd that he chose to include this second Tymes song on the album, given the hundreds of options he had. Perhaps it may have been simply that this song, like two other songs on this side, "Lonely Drifter" and "Wonderful Summer," had the sounds of surf and seabirds in the background and thus was in keeping with the album's vibe.

As mentioned in the write-up for "Ms. Grace," the group started out as the Latineers. Norm Burnett reminisced:

> *About that time there was a radio station contest for Tip Top bread. The deal was that you'd do your song, they'd play it on the radio and people would send them the end wrappers of the bread telling them who they liked in the contest. Well, we were nervous, and we didn't sing our best. But a promoter heard our audition when we were doing our tape for the radio program, and he told us to go to Cameo-Parkway records and he gave us the number. We called and set up an audition with Billy Jackson, the A&R man.*

For the audition, the group sang a song they had written called "As We Strolled," which would eventually be retitled "So Much in Love." In addition, "Bernie Lowe, the owner of Cameo-Parkway, didn't like our name, so he named us the Tymes. I don't know where he got it, but that's how our name came about."

With a new name, the newly titled "So Much in Love" was released in June 1963 and went all the way to #1. Burnett said the sounds of the seabirds and waves crashing at the beginning of the song were to give it a romantic feel, and after the song became successful, two other songs released that year, The O'Jays' "Lonely Drifter" (released in September) and Robin Ward's "Wonderful Summer" (released

in November) used similar sound effects, but neither charted as high as the Tymes' disk. Almost overnight, the group went from being unknowns who just happened to be on the same label with Chubby Checker, Bobby Rydell and the Dovells, to having a #1 record. They left Parkway in 1964, and the rest of their story is documented in the entry for "Ms. Grace."

2. "39-21-40 Shape" | The Showmen (1963)

Virginia natives the Showmen began as the Humdingers in the early 1950s, a group led by General Johnson (his given name). They recorded a few unreleased early sides for Atlantic in 1956 and then did a few demos and sent these to New Orleans–based producer Joe Banashak. Banashak agreed to work with them, and beginning in 1961, the newly rechristened Showmen recorded a number of sides on the Minit label with an up-and-coming talent in the recording industry named Allen Toussaint. Minit artists included Ernie K. Doe, Irma Thomas and Benny Spellman, so the Showmen were squarely in the middle of the burgeoning New Orleans R&B scene of the early 1960s.

The first of the Showmen's records released was "Country Fool" on Minit 362, but it was the record's flip side, "It Will Stand," that got the bulk of the airplay and went to #61 on the Hot 100. Their fifth Minit release was the now classic "39-21-40 Shape," a song Johnson had written when he was a teenager. Minit released the single with the much more provocative measurements "39-21-46" on the label, and Johnson told Jim Newsom that though Minit claimed it was a clerical and printing error, he didn't believe it. He said he thought it was to arouse interest, but though the label says "39-21-46," the lyrics of course always say "39-21-40 Shape."

A failure to sustain any chart success soon led to the group and the label parting ways, and most of the Minit recordings were eventually purchased by Imperial. In 1968, Johnson left to form the Chairmen of the Board; the Showmen continued recording, but no further chart records were forthcoming.

3. "Gotta Have Your Love" | Blue Swede (1974)

Blue Swede was a Swedish rock group during the 1970s, and if their single releases sound familiar—"Half Breed" (1973), "Hush" (1975), "Na Na Hey Hey Kiss Him Goodbye" (1978)—it's because they were cover versions. While covering other artists' music is generally not a recipe for success, their

1974 cover of the B.J. Thomas song "Hooked on a Feeling" was their big break when it went to #1.

"Gotta Have Your Love" was released as the B side of "Hooked on a Feeling" in Canada, New Zealand, Mexico and the United States, but it was never released as an A side. Although it has an early '70s soulful R&B sound, it's really not a strong enough song to have been a featured single release.

Again, this is the most puzzling entry on the album. It's a song very few people recognize now—with good reason.

4. "Lonely Drifter" | The O'Jays (1963)

Eddie Levert, Walter Williams, William Powell, Bobby Massey and Bill Isles were students at McKinley High School in Canton, Ohio, when they formed a group called the Triumphs in 1957. Renamed the Mascots, they recorded "Miracles" for the Apollo label in 1961, a single that reportedly impressed Cleveland DJ Eddie O'Jay enough that he advised the band about their music and they decided to rename themselves the O'Jays in his honor. In 1963, the group signed with Imperial, and their second single was 1963's "Lonely Drifter." The song opens with an intro similar to that the Tymes had used on their earlier 1963 release "So Much in Love," with the sound of seabirds and waves crashing on the beach. The O'Jays' version, led by Levert's mournful singing, was not as successful as the Tymes' ocean-intro release, which had gone to #1, but it did make the Hot 100 at #93 and as such was the group's first chart record.

The group followed up with a number of beach music classics recorded during the '60s, such as "I Dig Your Act," and "Deeper (In Love with You)." The group would really hit their stride in the 1970s, recording major Top 40 hits such as "Backstabbers" (#1 R&B), "Love Train" (#1 R&B and pop charts), "Used to Be My Girl" (#1 R&B) and many others.

5. "Wonderful Summer" | Robin Ward (1963)

Robin Ward was born Jackie Ward, and she did session and demo work and even released a few singles. But when she recorded a demo of "Wonderful Summer," the songwriters decided that instead of passing the song on to a more established artist they'd stick with Ward. They sped the song up to make her sound like a teenager (she was in her twenties at the time), and Jancik notes that they gave label credits to *Robin* Ward, the name of one of her daughters. It sold more than a million copies, becoming perhaps the biggest teen summer romance record of all time.

Though Ward never had another Top 40 record, her voice was later present on television shows, movies, and commercials. She sang on the themes for the shows *Flipper*, *Batman*, *Love, American Style* and *Maude* and was one of the female voices in the group on *The Partridge Family*. Her singing voice was overdubbed in movies for Natalie Wood, Linda Evans and Janet Leigh.

The album closed with Ward's sentimental homage to summer and romance, perhaps a fitting conclusion to the "lovers" side of the album due to the sound of surf and sea birds.

BILLY SMITH'S BEACH PARTY VOLUME 2: 14 MORE GREAT BEACH SOUNDS

Although the first *Beach Party* album had been produced and sold before the FBI intervened and a federal judge subsequently shut down the operation, Billy Smith and Deane Morris weren't off the hook just yet. As it transpired, not only had a second album been planned, but that the second album had already been pressed as well. "Only the first one was ever released," Morris told me. "But there was a second album."

Morris said, "When we talked to the judge about the first album, we'd already produced and made a second album, *Beach Party Volume 2*, and I told him they were already on the way. He said, 'I better not ever see those out on the street.' So I had them stored in my office for a long time, from 1979 on. In 1987, there was a big fire, and the building burned. The newspaper had a picture, and the only thing left was all these albums. But we never sold it."

Billy Smith's Beach Party Volume 2 had time-tested classics by the Swingin' Medallions, the O'Kaysions, Billy Ward and the Dominoes, the O'Jays, the Georgia Prophets, Arthur

Alexander and more. In retrospect, it is unfortunate Smith didn't obtain copyrights for the material. Like the first album, this was a solid collection, especially in that it contained songs that the earlier collections based on big-label catalogues never would have included. They also bridged a gap between those albums of the '60s and the onslaught of beach music collections that were just around the corner. In fact, Morris says they may have been the inspiration for some of those later collections. "I think Ripete learned from what we did wrong when they started producing albums the next year. They knew what they had to do to reproduce those songs. Today we know more about copyrighting songs than we ever have, but we didn't know that back then. Ripete did what we wanted to do, to go 1, 2, 3, 4, 5. But only our first one was ever released."

As before, what follows is directly from the album cover. Song titles and group credits are exactly as they appear on the album. As before, the liner notes said "created by Billy Smith" and listed Deane Morris as executive producer.

Billy Smith's Beach Party Volume 2: 14 More Great Beach Sounds
(No record company listed, 904027-2902)

Side 1
(For Dancers)

Double Shot of My Baby's Love, Swinging Medallions
Behold, Bob Meyer
Girl Watcher, O'Kaysions
60 Minute Man, Billy Ward and The Dominos
I Dig Your Act, O'Jays
I Got the Fever, Billy Scott and The Prophets
A Quiet Place, Garnet Mims and The Enchanters

Side 2
(For Lovers)

Anna, Arthur Alexander
One Nite Affair, O'Jays
In Paradise, Showmen
For the First Time, Billy and Barbara
She's Got It All Together, Harry Deal and The Galaxies
I Remember, Maurice Williams and The Zodiacs
Billy's Closing Theme,
I'm Going But I'll Be Back, Buster Brown

It's unfortunate that this album never hit the streets because it's one of the best collections, both of classics and near-classics, assembled on any album before then. But as good as the songs were, once again little thought was given to the sleeve's appearance—inconsistencies and misspellings abound, and the cover photo was the same stock picture as the first album. But bad or not, it's highly likely that for most people, the picture of the cover they see in this book is the closest they'll ever get to seeing one of the extremely rare copies of this unreleased album.

The Songs

Side 1
(For Dancers)
1. "Double Shot (of My Baby's Love)" | The Swingin' Medallions (1966)

The Medallions got together in 1962 at Lander College in Greenwood, South Carolina. John McElrath and his friends formed the band with their act based in rhythm and blues, and like many regional bands during the 1960s, they made their living lining up gigs to play across the South. McElrath and the group wanted to record "Double Shot," a huge regional hit that had been written and originally recorded by Dick Holler and the Holidays. "I had heard it played in Columbia at USC in the 1950s," McElrath told me. "It was a local hit when I was a teenager, and when we put our band together we started playing it too."

Eventually, the group was encouraged to record the song, and after a couple of misfires, they arrived at the final hit version: "We actually pulled

DOUBLE SHOT
(Of My Baby's Love)
(Fitter-Smith)

S M A S H

S-2033
YW1-37924
Lyresong Music
& Windsong Music
(BMI) 2:13

SWINGIN'
MEDALLIONS

in people off the street and had a big crowd in the studio to make background noise, and that party atmosphere gave us the sound we were looking for." Initially, the record was released on their For Sale label to be sold at their performances, but the record got some airplay and really started to take off. Soon they added the "Swingin'" moniker to the Medallions name, and history was made.

Smash records signed the group to distribute the record nationally, but they wanted some of the lyrics changed. McElrath said, "They didn't like some lines, like 'Woke up this morning, my head hurt so bad / The worst hangover that I ever had,' and made us change it to 'worst morning after that I ever had'—which was stupid, I thought." But even with the changes, it worked, and the single was released and became a million-seller, going all the way to #17 on the charts. After two more releases—"She Drives Me Out of My Mind" (pop #71) and a version of Bruce Channel's "Hey! Baby" called "Hey, Hey Baby"(did not chart)—the original band members started to go their separate ways, some going on to form the group Pieces of Eight, most going back to college to finish their educations. John McElrath passed away in 2018.

2. "Behold" | Bob Meyer and the Rivieras (1964)

Nat Speir and Charles Van Wagner formed the Rivieras in 1958, and in 1962 the group added a new lead vocalist in Bob Meyer. As their sound moved toward a '60s "blue-eyed soul" vibe, they recorded "Behold," a song written by Meyer and Speir, in a garage in Charlotte in 1963. The tune acquired an instant audience along the East Coast when released on the Casino label, and it was also released on the slightly more prestigious Lawn label, a subsidiary of Swan. Swan was the label where the Beatles had previously gone to #1 with "She Loves You," and perhaps through the connection between the two labels, legend has it that the Beatles heard and liked "Behold" and even considered recording it for a while during their early period when they were still covering songs by other writers. However, neither label's release of the Rivieras' "Behold" charted.

Although the group played with and opened for a number of famous acts over the years, including the Impressions, the Four Tops, the Temptations, the Platters and others, they never had any chart success nationally. Meyer didn't stay with the group long, though with some personnel changes, the Rivieras went on to record a number of singles. There continued to be many personnel changes throughout the '60s until the group folded in 1970.

3. "Girl Watcher" | The O'Kaysions (1968)

The Kays started in Wilson, North Carolina, and they mainly played in North and South Carolina, Georgia and Virginia, though by 1968 they had changed their name to the O'Kaysions. Their first recording under their new name was "Girl Watcher," the Wayne Pittman–penned tune they recorded for the tiny NorthState label in 1968. "We used to play down at Atlantic Beach a lot, and when we got back home people would say, 'Did you meet any girls this weekend?'" Pittman told me. "I'd say, 'I didn't meet any, but I sure do like to watch them.'" Eventually, one of the band members said, "'Wayne, you're the writer, why don't you write a song called 'I'm a Girl Watcher.'" I said, 'Okay, I will, I'll go back and write it, and I'll be back next week,' and that's exactly what I did. I wrote it in two nights that week."

The catchy tune was a hit regionally and came to the attention of ABC Records, which decided to pick up distribution. The song went to #5 on the charts, and eventually it reached gold record status with one million sales by December 1968. The group recorded an album, and a few of their songs garnered some notice on the beach music scene, but other than "Love Machine" (#76), nothing else the group recorded registered on the charts.

Eventually, Pittman decided it was time to get out of the music business.

> *That period was the beginning of the psychedelic and acid rock scene, and "Girl Watcher" had been an anomaly. Everywhere we played, the acid rock groups would go on, with all the noise and distortion, and there were the drugs all around, and I just didn't want to go in that direction. I knew I'd burn myself out if I stayed in it, so I just stopped performing.*

Wayne Pittman passed away in 2021.

4. "Sixty Minute Man" | Billy Ward and the Dominoes (1951)

Born in Savannah, Georgia, Robert L. Williams moved to Philadelphia, and according to *The Encyclopedia of Popular Music*, after military service he went to the Juilliard School of Music. He adopted the name Billy Ward, and his career plans were to work as a vocal coach and Broadway arranger. Ward soon formed his own vocal group called the Dominoes, so-called because the group consisted of White and Black singers. He disbanded the group in 1950, formed an all-Black group called the Ques, fired them and then formed another group of Ques consisting of Clyde McPhatter, Charlie White, William Lamont and Bill Brown. Renamed the Dominoes (again), they won a contest at the Apollo and appeared on *Arthur Godfrey's Talent Scouts Show* in 1950, which caught the attention of King Records. The powers at King convinced Ward that his group should try their hand at R&B.

Their third record was "Sixty Minute Man" with the deep-voiced Brown singing the lead. The double entendre lyrics led to the song being banned by many radio stations, though some simply saw it as a novelty record. Some critics claim it was the first rock-and-roll record, though Ward himself admitted he wasn't sure what it was exactly and that the song's distinctive sound came about almost by accident. "Sixty Minute Man" was voted the year's #1 record in the jazz and blues field by music writers and by the national jukebox operators and was #1 on the R&B charts, where it was in the Top 10 for months. It even crossed over and hit #17 on the early pre-*Billboard* pop charts, sold more than one million records and consequently bridged the gap between Black music and White music, which was extremely significant at the time.

Even though they followed "Sixty Minute Man" with several hits, Clyde McPhatter was tired of Ward's controlling ways and left the group. The Dominoes were lucky, however, in that despite the fact that they had lost the great Clyde McPhatter, waiting in the wings was another superior talent: Jackie Wilson (who at that point was still known as "Sonny" Wilson). Wilson sang lead on several other hits before he was fired by Ward for "misconduct." As the '50s wound down, the group's heyday was clearly behind them. There were frequent and numerous personnel changes in the ensuing years, although Ward tried to keep the group together into the late '60s. Billy Ward died in 2002.

5. "I Dig Your Act" | The O'Jays (1967)

While the first *Billy Smith's Beach Party* album had included the O'Jays' classic "Lonely Drifter," most beach music enthusiasts would probably agree this is actually the better song. In any event, it finally made it onto a beach music compilation album, even if this album was never actually released.

Larkin said the group came together in 1957 and became the O'Jays in honor of Cleveland DJ Eddie O'Jay. They recorded some non-charting sides before signing with Imperial in 1963. Their second single was 1963's "Lonely Drifter," which squeaked into the R&B Hot 100 at #93. The group followed up with more singles over the next two years on Imperial with only marginal success.

The O'Jays left Imperial and moved to Bell Records. There the group scored their first top ten hit on the R&B chart, a song called "I'll Be Sweeter Tomorrow (Than I Was Today)." It was the flip side, however, "I Dig Your Act," which would become one of the biggest beach music hits of the classic era. Written by Robert and Richard Poindexter, who wrote the Persuaders' hit "A Thin Line Between Love and Hate" and many other songs, this single is also considered a Top 500 northern soul song in England as well. Four more releases on Bell failed to equal their first release, however, and they moved to Kenny Gamble and Leon Huff's new Neptune label in 1969. That story is continued on side 2 under "One Night Affair."

6. "I Got the Fever" | Billy Scott and the Prophets (1968)

While the album cover says the group was Billy Scott and the Prophets, when the single was released in 1968, the group was called simply the Prophets. The group went by the name the Prophets in the mid- to late '60s, changed to the Georgia Prophets (1969), the Three Prophets (1971), then Billy Scott and the Prophets, then Billy Scott and the Georgia Prophets and so on. Most of the time people refer to them as Georgia Prophets for simplicity's sake, and as Billy Scott explained, that's the name fans gave them—and it stuck.

As one of the most dynamic and influential groups on the Carolina beach music scene, Prophets' frontman Billy Scott was born Peter Pendleton in Huntington, West Virginia. After being discharged from the army, he changed his name and, with his wife, Barbara, worked singing backup vocals in the Augusta, Georgia area. While in the studio

in 1965, local musician Tommy Witcher happened to hear them singing and asked the two to join his band, the Scottsmen. Soon the group changed their name to the Prophets, and eventually they had the chance to cut their first record, "Talk Don't Bother Me," for Delphi in 1966. Jubilee picked up the single for national distribution, and though it didn't chart, Jubilee also decided to release their next Delphi single, 1967's

77

"Don't You Think It's Time." This record failed to chart as well, but the group continued to play throughout Georgia and the Carolinas, hoping for their big break.

In 1968, Roy Smith wrote a song for them called "I Got the Fever." Billy Scott told me,

> *Roy called me and said, "You gotta come over to my house right now—I just wrote your next hit record." So I drove over to his house, and I sat down beside him at the piano. He started playing, and the hooks in that song just threw me back—"I love you, I love you, I love you yes I do." I went, "Oh man!" I mean, you know, it got me right then. Then he started playing the verses. It went back and forth like that and I thought, "Oh my God, this is going to be a great tune."*

Scott added that they played it for Witcher, and he arranged for them to go to Atlanta and record it on the Smash label. Though the song didn't make the national charts, it did sell well in the South.

Suddenly the group was bigger than ever, and that forced a change. Scott said,

> *We changed our name to the Georgia Prophets in 1969 for several reasons. There was a group called the Prophets in Florida that threatened to sue us, and there were also several other groups named the Prophets, and it was confusing for fans. We'd be booked somewhere and people would call and be told the Prophets were playing, and they'd ask, "Which Prophets?" Told it was us, people would say, "Oh, you mean the Georgia Prophets." So our fans really changed our name for us.*

With a new name, they were ready for a new release. The Georgia Prophets' story continues on side 2 with "For the First Time."

7. "A Quiet Place" | Garnet Mimms and the Enchanters (1964)

The artist known as Garnet Mimms was actually born "Garret" Mimms in Ashland, West Virginia, and Moore and Thornton note that Mimms had a strong background in the church and gospel music. Early on he sang with several groups, and while with the Gainors, they recorded 1958's "The Secret," which was a regional hit. Cameo picked up and released the first two Gainors' regional recordings hoping for a little national chart

action that was nevertheless elusive, and Mimms left to form another group, Garnet Mimms and the Enchanters. Almost from the start, the Enchanters weren't always the group backing up Mimms on those Garnet Mimms and the Enchanters singles, despite what the record label said. For example, on "Cry Baby," the group's biggest single—which went all the way to #4 on the pop charts and #1 on the R&B charts in 1963 and reportedly sold more than one million copies—the actual backing group was the Gospelaires, whose members included Dionne Warwick and Dee Dee Warwick. On the flip side of the record, however, "Don't Change Your Heart," it was indeed the Enchanters singing backup. "Baby Don't You Weep" (#30) and a cover of the Impressions' "For Your Precious Love" (#26) both made the pop and R&B Top 40. On the flip side of "One Girl," the real Enchanters *were* billed and *were* singing backup on the beach music classic, 1964's "A Quiet Place." Mimms's wailing song of a man is the beach song with perhaps the three most famous opening words—"Johnny, Johnny Dollar"—of all time. As a national record, it only went to #78.

The group was off to a good start, but perhaps the question over whether this was a one-man show or not led to Mimms decisively going out on his own in 1964. The Enchanters stayed together at first but disbanded in 1966. Mimms cut eight more records for United Artists, though only three charted and only one broke the Top 40. By the early '70s, Mimms found that he was still very popular on the growing UK northern soul scene, so he moved to England and continued to record well into the 1970s. Eventually, Mimms retired from the music industry and became a minister. In 1999, he received a Pioneer Award from the Rhythm and Blues Foundation.

Side 2
(For Lovers)
1. "Anna" | Arthur Alexander (1962)

Arthur Alexander Jr. (called "June" by his friends in reference to Jr.) was born in Florence, Alabama, and according to Richard Younger, his first success in the music business came when his group the Heartstrings sang on a few radio shows. He came to attention of Florence resident Tom Stafford, who along with Billy Sherrill and Rick Hall opened the Florence Alabama Music Enterprise in Muscle Shoals, now better known as FAME Studios. Alexander spent time in the studio and co-wrote a song called "She Wanna Rock," which was recorded by Amie Derkson in 1959. A year later, recording as June Alexander, he recorded another song he co-wrote, "Sally Sue Brown," which was later recorded by Bob Dylan. He then wrote another song that would become his second recording, "You Better Move On." It was recorded at FAME studios, and when it was released on Nashville's Dot label, the record finally brought him some notice. The song went to #24 on the pop charts and landed Alexander a booking on *American Bandstand*. It had the distinction of being the first national hit recorded in the state of Alabama and the studio's first hit of the many to follow. Like many of Alexander's recordings, it was covered by multiple artists, including the Rolling Stones, the Hollies and Chuck Jackson, among others.

After releasing the excellent but somewhat underappreciated "Soldier of Love," which was covered by the Beatles and others, his next recording was 1962's "Anna," written about his wife and their doomed relationship, which ultimately ended in divorce. "Anna" went to #68 on the pop charts and was reportedly one of John Lennon's favorite songs. Consequently, the Beatles also recorded it and in 1963 released their own version on the album *Please Please Me.* The Beatles eventually covered two other Alexander recordings, "A Shot of Rhythm and Blues" and "Where Have You Been," and with those and "Anna" and "Soldier of Love," it was clear, as Paul McCartney later said in a 1987 interview with Mark Lewisohn, that if the early "Beatles

80

ever wanted a sound, it was R&B....We wanted to be like Arthur Alexander." Despite the staggering influence of Alexander's music, "Anna" was his last record in the 1960s to make the pop charts. By the end of the decade, he was playing smaller venues, and Clifford Curry told me in an interview that the two of them "did a few gigs together in the Carolinas in the late 1960s," including the Beach Club in Myrtle Beach. He says Alexander was surprised at how popular his music still was among the beach music crowd. "He was really pleased by that," Curry said.

In popular music, Alexander's heartfelt recordings continued to inspire others, and "Burning Love" was covered by Elvis Presley. Another song Alexander wrote, "Every Day I Have to Cry Some," was first recorded by Steve Alaimo in 1962, then Dusty Springfield, the McCoys, the Bee Gees, Johnny Rivers and others before Alexander's own version went to #45 in 1975. His next recording, "Sharing the Night Together," did nothing until covered by Dr. Hook and the Medicine Show in 1978, when it peaked at #6.

On a personal level, however, Alexander's life was not so successful. Alexander divorced his wife, and his behavior became increasingly erratic. He often had to be tracked down in bars to perform, and on one occasion he walked off stage in the middle of a performance for no apparent reason. In the late 1970s, he inexplicably decided he was through with music and simply dropped out of sight. Alexander moved to Cleveland and spent most of the rest of his life in anonymity working as a bus driver and janitor, unknown even to his co-workers. In 1993, he recorded a comeback album, *Lonely Like Me*, but shortly thereafter he suffered a fatal heart attack and died at the age of fifty-three.

2. "One Night Affair" | The O'Jays (1969)

The Billy Smith albums are noteworthy for both being the first appearance of some of the greatest uncollected (at the time) beach music classics and at the same time for passing over more obvious choices for secondary hits by groups with bigger beach hits and a few songs that make no sense at all. "One Night Affair" is a decent song but never appeared on another compilation album.

With the O'Jays having left the Bell label (see side 1) after only marginal success, according to Moore and Thornton they migrated to Kenny Gamble and Leon Huff's new Neptune label in 1969. Though the label released only a little more than twenty singles in two years, the O'Jays were their most successful act, recording quality songs such as "Looky Looky" and "Christmas Just Ain't Christmas." Their first Neptune release was "One Night Affair," written by Gamble and Huff, who later wrote hits for them such as "Love Train," "Used to Be My Girl" and others. While those songs would all hit #1 on the R&B charts and all be Top 5 on the pop charts, as an early effort, "One Night Affair" only hit #68 on the pop charts and

#15 on the R&B charts. While it's a decent song, it is not a beach music classic by any means.

What is remarkable is that at this point the O'Jays hadn't had any sustainable chart success in more than a decade and had not once made the pop Top 40. When they signed with Gamble and Huff's new Philadelphia International label in 1972, their first release, "Backstabbers," brought them the success that had long eluded them. It went to #1 on the R&B charts and #3 on the pop charts, and after "Love Train" topped both the R&B and pop charts in 1973, the group was soon considered one of R&B's biggest acts. Five more singles topped the R&B charts over the next four years, followed by a sixth in 1978, "Used to Be My Girl." It was the group's last super hit, however, though nearly three dozen chart records followed.

3. "In Paradise" | The Showmen (1965)

As was explained in the write up for "39-21-40 Shape," the group began as the Humdingers in the early 1950s with frontman General Norman Johnson. Eventually, as the Showmen they landed with the Minit label, and the first of the Showmen's releases was "It Will Stand," which went to #61 on the Hot 100. Their fifth Minit release was the now classic "39-21-40 Shape," a song Johnson had written when he was a teenager. It did not chart, nor did any other Minit releases A failure to sustain any chart success soon led to the group and the label parting ways, and most of the

Minit recordings were eventually purchased by Imperial. "It Will Stand" actually charted again in 1964 on Imperial, this time going to #80 on the pop charts. The group eventually changed labels and recorded a song Johnson had written that gained some traction in beach music clubs, "In Paradise." Primarily based on its popularity in the Southeast, Swan picked it up along with a couple of other songs they had recorded; none of the Swan releases made the national charts.

In 1968, Johnson left to form the Chairmen of the Board. The Showmen continued recording, but no further chart records were forthcoming.

4. "For the First Time" | The Georgia Prophets (1969)

Sometimes artists can look back on a defining moment in their career and say, "This is when everything changed for me." Starting out, generally this means changed for the better, because if you're struggling to make a name for yourself change is generally positive. Sometimes that move into the spotlight is a recording that opens doors and gets your name out there. While to this point the Georgia Prophets had recorded on some decent mid-sized labels such as Jubilee and Smash, "For the First Time" was the song that almost saw their music on a national label unlike any other—Motown. Unfortunately, the operative word there is *almost*.

By 1969, the group was going by the Georgia Prophets. At about this same time, Roy Smith had written them a new song, a duet that emphasized the singing abilities of Billy and Barbara, "For the First Time." "[Roy] called up excited about the song saying 'I wrote you and Barbara a great

song,'" Billy Scott told me. "He asked, 'Can I play some of it for you over the phone? You'll sing this part, Barbara sings this part, then y'all sing this part together' So I listened and then I got excited about it too. We'd been looking for a really good duet." They recorded a demo, and it was impressive enough that they had a chance at their first really big break—Motown wanted to release the record nationally. At long last, the group seemed about to go from a regional band to national recording artists on the biggest stage possible.

But it was not to be. "Tommy [Witcher] made all the decisions and negotiated the record deals, and we were just singers in the band at the time," Scott told me. "Tommy said, 'I offered this to Motown, and they want it, but there really isn't much money in it for us.' I said, 'Okay, you're taking care of business so whatever you decide is what we'll go with.'" Instead, Witcher sold the song to Double Shot records in Hollywood, and Scott said, "Well, as bad as I wanted to go with Motown at the time, we were happy with Double Shot. I got a call from Irwin Zucker who was in charge of their promotions, and he let us know what a wonderful song it was, and that he was going to do everything he could to promote it." But despite the song's potential, it didn't make the *Billboard* Top 40, though it did reach #36 on the *Cash Box* R&B charts. Zucker called Scott again and told him, "Billy, I'm just taken aback with what's happening with this song. I don't understand it, it's a turntable record.' What he meant by that was that the DJ's loved the song, but it didn't sell like he wanted it to. Of course, we were really disappointed because we knew that it was a great tune." In retrospect, while Double Shot was a fine label, they were much smaller than Motown and perhaps Motown could have promoted the record better; no one will ever know.

At this point, they added another female vocalist to the group, Janet Helm, and Helm brought the group a song she had written, "California." The group was now signed to the Capricorn label, and although the song went on to be their most popular beach music song behind "I Got the Fever," once again the record didn't chart. A series of great beach classics followed, including "Nobody Loves Me Like You," "I Think I Really Love You" and "So Glad You Happened to Me," but none charted.

Unfortunately, as is often the case, a failure to find any sustained success led to the group splintering. Scott said he, Barbara and Janet felt like they were moving in one direction and the rest of the group was going in another. Ultimately Billy, Barbara and Janet started their own group in 1971. Witcher owned the rights to the Georgia Prophets name, but Billy, Barbara and Janet "didn't want to lose the name Prophets and lose our identity, so we went with the Three Prophets." Eventually, the group broke up, but Scott enjoyed continued success over the years as a solo artist, singing duets and with his band the Party Prophets until his death in 2012.

5. "She's Got It All Together" | Harry Deal and The Galaxies (1975)

Founders Harry and Jimmy Deal started the group in 1959, and their early appearances were doing gigs such as the Beta Club convention and 4-H Club contests. Perhaps most notable were their appearances at the Myrtle Beach Pavilion starting in 1960, where they reportedly set attendance records at the time. Their regional popularity interested record companies by the mid-1960s, and after their first release on the obscure Petal label in 1964, they next recorded "Bad Girl" for the higher profile Jubilee label in 1966. Despite successive recordings on the Laurie, Jubilee, SSS International and Atlantic labels over the next four years, none of their records made the national charts.

In 1968, they founded their own Galaxie III studios, and by 1970, they had their own label, Eclipse. Their first release on Eclipse was a song then-keyboardist Glen Fox had written called "I Still Love You." Though not a national hit, it was hugely successful in the Southeast, as was "She's Got it All Together," released on Eclipse just a few years later. This was by far the group's best known and most popular song on the beach club circuit. In the 1970s, they released covers of beach classics such as "Stay," "Ms. Grace" and "Hey Baby!" on Eclipse and occasionally saw releases on other labels as well.

The group's membership fluctuated a great deal over the years and at one time included influential Catalinas members Johnny and Gary Barker, as well as a number of Deal family members. Harry Deal passed away in 2017.

6. "I Remember" | Maurice Williams and the Zodiacs (1960)

To this point, Maurice Williams and the Zodiacs had received a fair amount of coverage on the previous four beach music albums, with both "May I" (*Beach Beat Vol. 2*) and "Stay" (*Summer Souvenirs*) having appeared. With "I Remember" appearing on this album, their three songs equaled the number of different songs included by the Clovers, Coasters and Willie Tee on the first five beach compilation albums.

As the entries for the group on the previous two albums explained, Maurice Williams and his group the Gladiolas first made the charts in 1957 with "Little Darlin'" on the Excello label. They soon changed their name to the Zodiacs, signed with Herald Records in New York and recorded another Williams composition, "Stay." The record went all the way to #1 pop charts.

"I Remember" was released as the follow-up to "Stay," and while "I'll Remember" is a great song, it was not a chart success and failed to register on a national scale. Four Herald singles followed "I Remember," and then they recorded singles on Soma, Atlantic, Sea-Horn, Intrigue, Candi, Vee Jay and then Dee-Su in 1965. There they recorded "May I," a monster regional hit that did not make the national charts. Releases on more than a half-dozen labels over the next decade and a half would produce no further hits. It is likely one of the songs Deane Morris referred to when he said Smith picked songs for

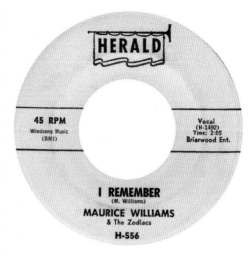

the albums that were popular in the late 1970s, because today it is not considered a beach music standard.

7. "I'm Going But I'll Be Back" | Buster Brown (1961)

If you asked anyone with a knowledge of beach music to name the genre's biggest acts, it's likely that Buster Brown wouldn't even make the top 100. Nevertheless, this is the second Buster Brown song to make the first five beach music albums, following "Fannie Mae" on *Summer Souvenirs*. Like "Fannie Mae," "I'm Going" seems to have been included more as a beneficiary from circumstances rather than its standing as a beach classic.

Brown first recorded the #1 hit "Fannie Mae" on the Fire label (see *Summer Souvenirs*), but other than two singles, 1960's "Is You Is or Is You Ain't My Baby" and 1961's "Sugar Babe," further chart success eluded him. The flip side of "Sugar Babe" was this song, "I'm Going—But I'll Be Back." The song never made the charts and was not a beach music standard and owes its inclusion here to the fact that during the 1970s it received a fair amount of airplay from Smith, who would play it at the end of his radio show—so much so that here it is listed as "Billy's Closing Theme."

Brown left Fire shortly thereafter, and a series of singles during the 1960s on small labels brought no further success. His music reached a new generation of listeners when "Fannie Mae" was on the *American Graffiti* soundtrack in 1973, but no new recordings followed. Brown passed away in Brooklyn in 1976.

5

BEACH MUSIC GOES NATIONAL: WARNER BROTHERS' *OCEAN DRIVE VOLUME 1*

WARNER SPECIAL PRODUCTS 2520, 1980

*I*n 1979, it had been almost thirteen years since the first Atlantic *Beach Beat* album had been released, and in terms of beach music available to the masses, very little had changed. A good barometer is a survey that was published in 1979 in Chris Beachley's *It Will Stand* magazine, a magazine that covered beach music and anything beach music related. The magazine featured old-style beach music from the '40s, '50s and early '60s, as well as then-current releases by regional bands that had come out in the late 1960s and the 1970s.

In 1979–80, the magazine ran a poll and subsequently offered the following list of the Top 50 beach music hits of all time as voted on by fans.

1. Billy Ward & the Dominoes, "Sixty Minute Man" (1951)
2. The Tymes, "Ms. Grace" (1974)
3. Willie Tee, "Thank You John" (1965)
4. The Catalinas, "Summertime's Calling Me" (1975)
5. The Showmen, "39-21-40 Shape" (1963)
6. Jimmy Ricks and the Ravens, "Green Eyes" (1955)
7. Garnet Mimms and the Enchanters, "A Quiet Place" (1964)
8. Barbara Lewis, "Hello Stranger" (1963)

9. The Clovers, "Nip Sip" (1955)
10. Tony Clarke, "The Entertainer" (1964)
11. The Platters, "With This Ring" (1967)
12. Maurice Williams and the Zodiacs, "Stay" (1960)
13. The Clovers, "One Mint Julep" (1952)
14. Doris Troy, "Just One Look" (1963)
15. The Tams, "I've Been Hurt" (1965)
16. Willie Tee, "Walking Up a One Way Street" (1965)
17. The Platters, "Washed Ashore (On a Lonely Island in the Sea)" (1967)
18. The Embers, "Far Away Places" (1969)
19. The Tams, "Be Young, Be Foolish, Be Happy" (1968)
20. The Georgia Prophets, "I Got the Fever" (1968)
21. The Temptations, "My Girl" (1965)
22. Lenny O'Henry, "Across the Street" (1964)
23. Bruce Channel, "Hey! Baby" (1962)
24. Marvin Gaye, "Stubborn Kind of Fellow" (1962)
25. The Embers, "I Love Beach Music" (1979)
26. The Trammps, "Hold Back the Night" (1975)
27. Billy Stewart, "I Do Love You" (1965)
28. The Drifters, "Under the Boardwalk" (1964)
29. The Chairmen of the Board, "(You've Got Me) Dangling on a String" (1970)
30. The Platters, "I Love You 1,000 Times" (1966)
31. The Georgia Prophets, "California" (1970)
32. The Artistics, "I'm Gonna Miss You" (1966)
33. The Drifters, "I've Got Sand in My Shoes" (1964)
34. The Coasters, "Zing! Went the Strings of My Heart" (1958)
35. Jackie Wilson, "(Your Love Keeps Lifting Me) Higher and Higher" (1967)
36. The Checkers, "White Cliffs of Dover" (1953)
37. The Radiants, "It Ain't No Big Thing" (1965)
38. The Showmen, "It Will Stand" (1961)
39. Deon Jackson, "Love Makes the World Go Round"(1965)
40. Mary Wells, "My Guy" (1964)
41. The Globetrotters, "Rainy Day Bells" (1970)
42. Billy Stewart, "Sitting in the Park" (1965)
43. The Chairmen of the Board, "Everything's Tuesday" (1970)
44. Wynonie Harris, "Good Rockin' Tonight" (1948)
45. Maurice Williams and the Zodiacs, "May I" (1965)
46. Hank Ballard and the Midnighters, "Work With Me Annie"(1954)
47. The Four Tops, "I Just Can't Get You Out of My Mind" (1974)

48. The "5" Royales, "Think" (1957)
49. Archie Bell and the Drells, "I Can't Stop Dancing" (1968)
50. Billy Stewart, "Fat Boy" (1962)

IF WE TAKE THE *It Will Stand* list as the barometer of the most popular and best beach music recorded by 1980 (and I think it is an exceptional and quite accurate list), the following songs had been available on beach music compilation albums at that point:

On Atlantic's first *Beach Beat* album, "Thank You John," "One Mint Julep," "Just One Look," "Walking Up a One-Way Street" and "Zing! Went the Strings of My Heart," which was a pretty good start. *Beach Beat Vol. 2* contained "Hello Stranger," "Nip Sip," "The Entertainer," "Across the Street," "May I" and "Fat Boy." Of *Summer Souvenirs'* thirteen songs, only "Stay" was on the list. That means that of the Top 50 beach music songs, only a dozen had been widely available at some point on nationally released LPs and more than a decade earlier at that. Though Billy Smith's first *Beach Party* album was not nationally released, it was available in some coastal areas, and so "Ms. Grace," "39-21-40 Shape" and "Rainy Day Bells" could be added to the list, bringing us to fifteen. Because Billy Smith's second album was never released, those songs were still unavailable on beach music compilation albums. Consequently, in 1980, the number of the *It Will Stand* revered beach classics available to album buyers stood at just fifteen out of fifty.

Realistically, though, even that wasn't true. Ironically, the albums that had rescued some of the old beach classics from a graveyard of largely forgotten and unavailable songs now themselves needed to be rescued. "By now we were in a different era," Ed Weiss told me, "and those Atlantic albums hadn't been available for years." In 1979, the beach music on LPs industry was basically back to square one. But Weiss, Barrie Bergman and Larry Crockett decided to seize the opportunity, and thus was born *Ocean Drive Volume 1.*

"My friend (Barrie Bergman) was by then the president of the *Record Bar*, and Larry Crockett was a good friend. Larry was a

beach music lover had a syndicated show at the time from Raileigh. He had made contacts at Warner Special Products, so we had money, contacts and relationships with the WEA people." The Atlantic Records catalogue was now a part of Warner Brothers, and since 1972 the company had been known as Warner-Elektra-Atlantic—WEA for short. "It wasn't just Atlantic Records anymore, and all that Atlantic music belonged to WEA, and Larry had contacts there. Barrie knew WEA people for current music, but he didn't know any of the licensing people. WEA was so big that the people Barrie dealt with didn't have anything to do with the licensing people, so that was Larry Crockett's job, and he did a great job getting all that stuff licensed for us." Weiss said the WEA conglomerate meant that things had changed as far as the available catalogues too. "Because it was WEA, the library was bigger, and there were new songs that had become beach music as beach music had changed and so we had a lot more songs to choose from."

How they sold the music also changed. "We had this brilliant idea to sell this music on television," and Larry and Barrie "developed television commercials for it. I was very passive in that, quite frankly," Weiss said. "Barrie made sure I got taken care of on that deal, but it was really Larry and Barrie who did all of it. Larry was the one to help get the songs and Barrie was the one to set up the television deals." It sounded like a recipe for success: make this long-unavailable music available once again and concentrate on marketing it using television commercials. Many of the songs had been national hits at some point, so even if someone wasn't familiar with beach music, they might buy the album because it was a good oldies collection. They initially produced three great albums in 1980 and 1981 containing seventy-two excellent songs. More importantly, the *It Will Stand* list of the fifty all-time beach classics jumped from fifteen available songs to thirty-six, with twenty-one new classics becoming available on a beach compilation album for the first time ever. While *Ocean Drive Volume 1* contained only four songs from the *It Will Stand* list new to compilation albums—"Ms. Grace," "Hold Back the Night," "Under the Boardwalk" and "I've Got Sand in My Shoes"—it also contained twelve songs from the list that had been on those first two Atlantic albums years ago, meaning roughly a third of the all-time greats were on Volume 1 alone.

No doubt due to the national reputations enjoyed by Crockett, Bergman and Weiss, as well as their major marketing push, for the first time beach music albums were receiving national attention. *Billboard* writer Robyn Wells said Beach Beat Records (as Crockett, Bergman and Weiss were calling their new venture) was "working towards strong penetration east of the Mississippi and on the west coast." In a 1982 review of *Ocean Drive Volumes 1–3* in the *San Francisco Examiner*, Joel Selvin defined beach music as music enjoyed where "swimming, sunning, drinking and dancing to rhythm and blues records are the order of the day," which certainly sounded appealing no matter where you lived. So with the national attention; the seasoned promotional and creative team of Crockett, Bergman and Weiss; and the finest collection of beach music ever assembled on LPs, it seemed to be a sure thing.

Except that it wasn't. As unbelievable as it seems today, Weiss said basically the albums were a failure. "We had a problem, and we didn't understand this at the time": the use of CODs through the post office—"collect on delivery." The idea was that you'd order an album and the buyer would pay for it when it was delivered. The problem was that in a pre–debit card world, when not everyone had credit cards, a lot of people "had the money to pay for it, but it depended on when the product got delivered." If it was around payday, fine. If not, it could be a problem and the product would be returned. "The returns on the stuff we sold because the albums were undeliverable or they were unable to collect were unbelievable." It was so bad, in fact, that "we never made any money on the thing. Barrie finally bought what was left and bought us out and sold them in his Record Bar stores. That's how those two or three went, but I think the Record Bar did finally sell them all though." Bergman also got them into Pickwick, Stark, National Records and Tapes, Musicland, and other long forgotten chains that sold vinyl in the early '80s. Although *Billboard* noted in 1981 that Beach Beat Records was "claiming sales of 35,000 and 21,000" for the first two *Ocean Drive* albums, considering the national marketing, including television commercials and print ads and promotions, that number may have still seemed modest. As Ripete would prove the same year, more than 100,000 in sales—just for their *Beach Beat Volume 1*—was certainly possible. In any event, it was a great collection, even if Beach Beat Records ran its course when the albums were sold out, while Ripete Records lasted more than forty years.

OCEAN DRIVE VOLUME 1
(WARNER SPECIAL PRODUCTS 2520, 1980)

Side 1
1. "Think a Little Sugar," Barbara Lewis
2. "One Way Love," The Drifters

3. "You're the Boss," Laverne Baker and Jimmy Ricks
4. "Hold Back the Night," The Trammps
5. "Zing! Went the Strings of My Heart," The Coasters
6. "Teasin' You," Willie Tee

Side 2

1. "Ms. Grace," The Tymes
2. "Just One Look," Doris Troy
3. "Under the Boardwalk," The Drifters
4. "Nip Sip," The Clovers
5. "Dear Lover," Mary Wells
6. "Money Honey," Clyde McPhatter and the Drifters

Side 3

1. "(There's Gonna Be A) Showdown," Archie Bell and the Drells
2. "Searchin'," The Coasters
3. "Up on the Roof," The Drifters
4. "Slip Away," Clarence Carter
5. "Drinkin' Wine Spo-Dee-O-Dee," "Stick" McGhee
6. "Across the Street," Lenny O'Henry

Side 4

1. "Soul Man," Sam and Dave
2. "Mama He Treats Your Daughter Mean," Ruth Brown
3. "Tighten Up," Archie Bell and the Drells
4. "One Mint Julep," The Clovers
5. "Walking Up a One Way Street," Willie Tee
6. "I've Got Sand in My Shoes," The Drifters

THE ALBUM'S LINER NOTES had the usual homage to the South and what beach music was and went on to say "Produced by Eddie Weiss and Larry Crockett" and special thanks to, among others, "Barrie Bergman, Chris Beachley and "*It Will Stand*" Magazine."

The Songs

As noted earlier, some of the songs had appeared on the first two *Beach Beat* albums, as this album also drew almost exclusively from the Atlantic catalogue. All of the singles had been originally released on Atlantic or Atco except for "Soul Man," which was on Stax but Atlantic had the distribution rights to, and "Hold Back the Night" and "Ms. Grace," two of the hottest beach songs of the '70s.

Songs that have already been discussed are so noted below.

Side I
I. "Think a Little Sugar" | Barbara Lewis

This track was previously on Atlantic's *Beach Beat*. See that album for details about the song.

2. "One Way Love" | The Drifters (1964)

For background on the group's early years, see the entries for "Money Honey," "There Goes My Baby" and "Honey Love" in chapter 1 on *Beach Beat*.

The Drifters, who recorded for Atlantic in the '50s and '60s, produced so many songs that qualified as beach music, after the three that had appeared on *Beach Beat* there were still many songs left to choose from. "One Way Love," a very good song, was the first of five Drifters songs on this album. Still, it was a somewhat puzzling choice given the extensive Drifters' catalogue: as music critic Marv Goldberg said, "Can't say that I remember 'One Way Love' at all, but someone bought it."

After Ben E. King left the Drifters in 1960, the group had a fluid line-up of lead singers over the next few years, including Johnny Lee Williams and Rudy Lewis. Johnny Moore, who had been with the group in the 1950s before being drafted, had returned to the group in 1963, and he sang lead vocals on "One Way Love," a song written by Bert Berns (a.k.a. Bert Russell) and Jerry Ragovoy. Berns had written hits such as the Jarmels' "A Little Bit of Soap" and the Exciters' "Tell Him" prior to "One Way Love" and went on to write or co-write songs such as "I Want Candy" by the Strangeloves, "Hang on Sloopy" by the McCoys and others. Jerry Ragovoy also wrote "Time Is on My Side" by the Rolling Stones and "Piece of My Heart," which Janis Joplin made famous, and he also wrote songs recorded by Elvis Presley, Dusty Springfield, Dionne Warwick and Barry White.

As for "One Way Love," which *Cash Box* magazine called "a pulsating" song recorded "in their very commercial manner," it was not a big hit, going only to #56 on the pop chart and #12 on the R&B chart. While it was a good song and did get some play in beach clubs, it was never a mainstay of beach music playlists.

3. "You're the Boss" | Laverne Baker and Jimmy Ricks (1961)

Delores Lavcrn Baker was seventeen when she began singing in Chicago clubs, and by 1947, she had released a few singles on RCA and National but none charted. Baker signed with Atlantic Records, and while her first two records did nothing, the third, 1954's "Tweedlee Dee," was a R&B (#4) and pop (#14) hit. Baker followed up "Tweedlee Dee" with several chart records before recording "Jim Dandy," which sold more than one million units and earned a gold record while topping the R&B charts for eighteen weeks. By this point, she was famous enough that she was appearing in rock-and-roll films while continuing to have records on both charts. While she had her last Top 10 pop hit in 1958, between 1958 and 1961, she had five Top 40 R&B singles and seven Top 100 pop singles before recording "You're the Boss" with Jimmy Ricks in 1961.

Ricks's career, however, was in a very different place in 1961. Born James Thomas Ricks, he founded the Ravens, who in 1947 signed with National Records. Their second record, the standard "Ol' Man River," hit #10 on the R&B charts and was followed by several more chart records. They began having personnel changes in the late 1940s, signing with Columbia and Mercury before Jubilee. In 1955, they recorded "Green Eyes" (a highly regarded beach song that comes in at #6 on the *It Will Stand* Top 50 list), and then in 1956 Ricks left the group to go out on his own. As a solo act, Ricks went on to cut unsuccessful sides on a variety of small labels, and he also did a number of duets, including "You're the Boss" with Lavern Baker in 1961. The song's pedigree was great, as it had been written by Jerry Leiber and Mike Stoller, who have already been cited here for writing "Searchin'" and "There Goes My Baby" on the first *Beach Beat* album, but who had also written #1 hits by Elvis ("Hound Dog" and "Jailhouse Rock"), Wilbert Harrison ("Kansas City") and others. In this case, however, the Leiber and Stoller–penned tune made it to only #81 on the pop charts.

Sadly, this single was the last recording of note for Ricks, who died in 1974. Baker had very little chart success after this record and passed away from heart disease in 1997.

4. "Hold Back the Night" | The Trammps (1975)

Formed in Philadelphia as the Volcanos, the group signed with the Artic label and saw their second record, "Storm Warning," peak at #33 on the R&B charts in 1965. They subsequently recorded a single as the Body Motions, and later as the Moods they recorded several singles to no avail. After some personnel changes, the group re-formed in 1972 and considered several names before settling on the Trammps, which founder Earl Young said he chose because "they were kind of raggedy when I first got them together, so the Trammps was a pretty appropriate name."

The Trammps cut a couple of old standards on Buddah with moderate success, including "Zing! Went the Strings of My Heart" and "Sixty Minute Man." They left Buddah and signed with Atlantic in 1975, but Buddah released a song they still had the publishing rights to called "Hold Back the Night." The 1975 release was an obvious reworking of an instrumental called "Scrub Board" they had recorded as a B side in 1972. With Jimmy Ellis singing a powerful lead, "Hold Back the Night" came in at #35 and became the group's first Top 40 pop record and Top 10 R&B hit. Like so many beach music hits, in England it did even better and peaked at #5.

Now under contract to Atlantic, subsequent tunes would be more disco-based. Singles including "That's Where the Happy People Go" and their mega-hit "Disco Inferno" became disco classics, and the group had more than a dozen further releases on Atlantic, Venture and Philly Sound through 1983. But once disco died, the group was not as popular, and by the 1990s the group had split up. Lead singer Jimmy Ellis died in 2012.

5. "Zing! Went the Strings of My Heart" | The Coasters

This track was previously on Atlantic's *Beach Beat*. See that album for details about the song.

6. "Teasin' You" | Willie Tee

This track was previously on Atlantic's *Beach Beat Vol. 2*. See that album for details about the song.

Side 2

1. "Ms. Grace" | The Tymes

This track was previously on *Billy Smith's Beach Party: 10 Great Beach Classics*. See that album for details about the song.

2. "Just One Look" | Doris Troy

This track was previously on Atlantic's *Beach Beat*. See that album for details about the song.

3. "Under the Boardwalk" | The Drifters (1964)

One thing the first *Ocean Drive* collection did was to correct the obvious failure to previously include some of the Drifters' songs that had been resonating with beach music lovers for quite some time. In essence, these were first "beach music about the beach" songs, long before the Catalinas did "Summertime's Calling Me" or the Chairmen of the Board did "On the Beach." "Under the Boardwalk" and "I've Got Sand in My Shoes" are literally about the beach, and granted, while it had been true when Ed Weiss said of those first *Beach Beat* albums "'Under the Boardwalk' was almost a current....That stuff wasn't beach music yet," by 1980 it decidedly was.

After "One Way Love" reached its chart peak, the Drifters' next recording was "Under the Boardwalk." Rudy Lewis and Johnny Moore had been alternating lead vocals on the Drifters' recordings, and for this record, Lewis was scheduled to sing lead. According to Marv Goldberg, on the way in to the studio Johnny Moore ran into Sylvia Vanterpool, one-half of the duo Mickey and Sylvia. Vanterpool apparently told Moore, "Thank God it isn't you," though Moore was surprised and asked what she meant. She told him she'd heard one of the Drifters had died the night before, and as he later learned, it had been Rudy Lewis. How he died is unclear, but it's generally accepted that it was probably a drug overdose. He was twenty-seven years old.

Surprisingly, the saddened members of the Drifters showed up to record that day anyway. Most of the lead vocal duties for the recordings scheduled for that day had to be shuffled, and Moore sang lead on "Under the Boardwalk." It has often been said "Under the Boardwalk"—a perfect beach song, mentioning the sea, the sun, blankets on the sand and young love—has a mournful feel to it, and of course Lewis's death is the reason why. The song was written by Kenny Young and Arthur Resnick, both of whom were just starting to find real success as songwriters. Young wrote songs for a number of artists, including Herman's Hermits and the Seekers, and Resnick had written for Gene McDaniels and would write or co-write "Good Lovin'" by the Rascals and "Yummy Yummy Yummy" and other songs by the Ohio Express. "Under the Boardwalk" was a hit that resonated with radio listeners everywhere, peaking at #4 on the pop charts. Surprisingly, it was the group's last Top 10 pop hit in America.

4. "Nip Sip" | The Clovers

This track was previously on Atlantic's *Beach Beat Vol. 2*. See that album for details about the song.

5. "Dear Lover" | Mary Wells (1966)

Though Mary Wells was represented on the *It Will Stand* Top 50 list by "My Guy," "Dear Lover" was the first Wells tune to appear on a beach music compilation album. However, that may have had more to do with Motown owning the rights to her better-known earlier songs, as Berry Gordy was notoriously hesitant to license his music to others. At this point, no Motown songs had appeared on a beach music compilation album.

Detroit-born Mary Esther Wells was singing in nightclubs by the time she was seventeen, and a friend arranged for her to meet Motown founder Berry Gordy. Wells pitched him a song she had written called "Bye, Bye, Baby," and Gordy had her record it for him. The song went to #45 on the pop charts and #8 on the R&B charts and made Wells one of Gordy's first stars.

Gordy had Smokey Robinson write some songs for Wells, including "The One Who Really Loves You," followed by "You Beat Me to the Punch," which became her first R&B #1 record. When she recorded the Robinson-penned 1964 hit "My Guy," it went all the way to #1 on the pop charts. Only twenty-one years old, she was already the biggest Motown star and the first Motown artist nominated for a Grammy. She toured with the Beatles, who said she was their favorite American singer. Shockingly, however, "My Guy" would be her last recording for Motown.

By 1964, Wells was unhappy with Motown because she felt the label was spending their resources promoting up-and-coming acts such as the Supremes and the Four Tops rather than on her. This was a feeling shared by other groups at Motown, and in fact, Bobbie Smith of the Spinners told me in an interview,

> *We had some real good stuff at Motown that wasn't getting promoted....* [DJs] *played* [our songs] *and then all of a sudden they weren't playing* [them] *any more. They said, "Marvin Gaye has a new song, and we got orders from Motown to take yours off and put his on." So they'd play Marvin's or whoever else's Motown was pushing and take ours off.*

Wells apparently felt Motown was doing this to her music too, and eventually Wells voided her contact by pointing out she'd signed it as a seventeen-year-old minor. She was done at Motown, and it ended bitterly.

Almost immediately, 20th Century Fox signed her for an amount that was reported to have been as much as $500,000 and promised to make her a movie star too. Morty Craft, head of the record label, told Charlie Gillett it was all a lie just to get her to sign. "Why should I feel sorry I tricked her?" he told Gillett. "If she's so crazy with overblown ambition she deserves what she gets." She didn't become a movie star, and only one record there made the pop Top 40. Next she signed with Atco, where she was able to work with the very capable Carl Davis (who worked with the Artistics, Jackie Wilson and Major Lance) and Gerald Sims (The Radiants, Billy Stewart, Jerry Butler). Together they created "Dear Lover," her first and only successful single for the label. With its strings and brass it was different from her Motown recordings, and "Dear Lover" went to #51 on the Hot 100 and to #6 on the R&B charts. But despite the promising beginning, only one more single on Atco made the pop Hot 100. She later had releases on Jubilee, Reprise and Epic—but none did well—and "Dear Lover" remained the highest-charting record of her post-Motown career. Her private life was in turmoil as well, as she was twice divorced, had a failed suicide attempt and was addicted to cocaine and then heroin. She also smoked, and in 1990, she was diagnosed with laryngeal cancer. It was too much for her fragile health, as she had also had both meningitis and tuberculosis previously. She died in 1992 at the age of forty-nine.

6. "Money Honey" | Clyde McPhatter and the Drifters

This track was previously on Atlantic's *Beach Beat*. See that album for details about the song.

Side 3
1. "(There's Gonna Be A) Showdown" | Archie Bell and the Drells (1968)

It's understandable that Archie Bell and the Drells hadn't appeared on a beach music album previously, as their hits had come after the first two *Beach Beat* albums had been released. With *Ocean Drive Volume I*, however, their music finally came to a compilation album.

Archie Bell formed his first group in 1966, and in 1967, they recorded a couple of sides for the Ovide label, including "Tighten Up." But soon Bell was drafted, and just as he was being inducted into the army, "Tighten Up" took off in the South. The record was picked up by Atlantic and hit #1 nationally (more on that record later). Subsequently, the army allowed Bell to go on leave to record and perform from time to time, and on one such trip he met Kenny Gamble and Leon Huff. The group recorded their song "I Can't Stop Dancing," and in 1968, it went to #9 on the pop charts, perhaps because it closely followed the same formula as their previous hit. The group followed that with "There's Gonna Be a Showdown," another Gamble and Huff composition, which was based on "dance competitions [where] they'd have this thing called a 'showdown,'" Bell told me. "They'd form a big circle and put money in a hat and the one who ended up winning would win the pot. Well, every time you would win, you'd put a notch on your shoe. That's why the words to the song say 'I got ten notches, on my shoes'—that's where that came from." The song peaked at #21 for his third big hit of 1968.

In 1969, Bell was mustered out of the army, and the group also released "Girl You're Too Young" and "My Balloon's Going Up." They both charted, but neither did as well as their usual dance-themed songs had done. The group left Atlantic in 1972 and signed with the Glades label. Despite the fact that their biggest song for the label, "Dancing to Your Music," was, as Bell said, "a great song, one of my favorites," it went to only #61 on the pop charts and #11 on the R&B charts. Thereafter they signed with Gamble and Huff's TSOP subsidiary of Philadelphia International. "I Could Dance all Night" went to #25 on the R&B charts in 1975, and over the next four years, they had R&B chart hits twice more on TSOP and then four times on Philadelphia International. In 1979, they decided to call it quits as a group.

2. "Searchin'" | The Coasters

This track was previously on Atlantic's *Beach Beat*. See that album for details about the song.

3. "Up on the Roof" | The Drifters (1962)

One of the group's most highly regarded songs, "Up on the Roof," though not really about the beach, was certainly beach-like. As *Rolling Stone* said in 1985, it is "a breezy summertime song for city dwellers whose only getaways were the tar beaches at the top of their buildings."

The song was written by Gerry Goffin and Carole King, who had written the 1961 hit "Some Kind of Wonderful" as well. According to Sheila Weller, King came up with idea for the song while driving her car and originally called it "My Secret Place." It was Goffin who renamed it, and he later claimed it was his favorite song that he ever wrote. Recorded in 1962 with Rudy Lewis singing lead, by 1963, it had hit #5 on the pop chart and #4 on the R&B chart.

The song has come to be recognized as one of the greatest hits of popular music, most notably earning praise as one of the Rock and Roll Hall of Fame's *500 Songs That Shaped Rock and Roll.* ("Money Honey" and "There Goes My Baby" also made the list.)

4. "Slip Away" | Clarence Carter (1968)

Clarence Carter was educated at the Alabama School for the Blind, where he learned to play the guitar and piano. He graduated from Alabama State College with a degree in music and formed a band that did backup work for Otis Redding and Gene Chandler. Carter was at Rick Hall's Muscle Shoals–based FAME Studios to record some songs when Hall heard him singing, and eventually Carter recorded several songs on Hall's own Fame label, beginning a working relationship that would last a number of years.

Carter eventually signed with Atlantic, and in 1968, he had his first hit for the label, "Slip Away." A song of heartbreak and lost love, the song went #2 on the R&B chart and #6 on the pop chart in 1968 and earned him a gold record. It is not generally considered a standard beach song and perhaps earned a place on this album because some shaggers liked it and it was part of the Atlantic catalogue.

In 1970, Carter recorded "Patches," written by Chairmen of the Board frontman General Johnson, which would go on to be his biggest hit. Carter never had another hit as big as "Patches" or "Slip Away," as the early '70s gave way to the disco movement. He signed with the Atlanta-based Ichiban label in the 1980s, where he would be most famous for the off-color single

"Strokin'," which the *New York Times* claimed had sold 1.5 million records by 1998.

Carter is a member of the Alabama and Georgia Music Hall of Fame.

5. "Drinkin' Wine Spo-Dee-O-Dee" | "Stick" McGhee"

This track was previously on Atlantic's *Beach Beat*. See that album for details about the song.

6. "Across The Street" | Lenny O'Henry

This track was previously on Atlantic's *Beach Beat Vol. 2*. See that album for details about the song.

Side 4
1. "Soul Man" | Sam and Dave (1967)

Sam Moore and Dave Prater were casual acquaintances on the gospel circuit who sang together one night at a nightclub and began working together after that. After Atlantic's Jerry Wexler met them, he signed them to Atlantic and had them record for Memphis-based Stax Records, with whom Atlantic had a distribution deal. At the time, Stax had the greatest group of singers, songwriters and musicians found anywhere except perhaps Motown, and Sam and Dave benefited from working with and associating with Isaac Hayes, Booker T. & the M.G.'s, Otis Redding and many others.

Starting with their third Stax release, "You Don't Know Like I Know" in 1966, they were a constant presence on the R&B charts and often the pop charts as well. Their biggest hit was "Soul Man," co-written by Isaac Hayes and David Porter, which was an R&B #1 and hit #2 on the pop charts in 1967. They won the Grammy for "Best Performance—Rhythm & Blues Group" for "Soul Man" that year, and it was also their first gold record.

Despite all the popularity and accolades, this is not the kind of song you'd expect the find on a beach music album. It was inspired by race riots in Detroit, so it certainly isn't a typical beach song. It may have had something to do with the popularity of the 1980 movie *The Blues Brothers*, which included a cover version of the song. In short, while this a classic R&B song and a great party song, it isn't typically considered a beach song.

2. "Mama He Treats Your Daughter Mean" | Ruth Brown (1953)

Ruth Alston Weston got her start singing in the Methodist church, and when she was sixteen, she told her parents she was going to visit an uncle and took a bus to New York to sing at an amateur contest at the Apollo Theater. She won first prize, and soon she was singing part time while she finished high school. After graduation, she eventually she got a job in Washington, D.C.'s Crystal Caverns jazz, and after Atlantic Records' founder Ahmet Ertegun saw her perform, he offered her a contract with his label.

Her first release in 1949, "So Long," went to #6 on the R&B charts, and in 1950, "Teardrops from My Eyes," written by Rudy Toombs (who also wrote the Clovers' "One Mint Julep") was #1 for eleven weeks, becoming the label's first million-seller. Brown followed "Teardrops" with successive Top 10 records, and during her impressive run, she stayed on the R&B charts for 149 weeks with five #1 hits. Her biggest #1 hit was the 1953 Johnny Wallace and Herb Lance composition "(Mama) He Treats Your Daughter Mean." Wallace and Lance claimed to have heard a blues singer on an Atlanta street corner singing for change, and he dropped the line into one of his songs. Wallace and Lance wrote a slow ballad around the line but changed the tempo to fit Brown's style. Brown did not like the song (she told author Chip Deffaa it was "the silliest mess I'd ever heard") and supposedly recorded it only because Wallace and Lance were her friends. It became her biggest hit, and it crossed over onto the pop charts, where it hit #23.

Brown had seventeen more R&B hits through 1959 before leaving Atlantic in 1961 and signing with Phillips, then Decca and then Mainstream, but after she left Atlantic, the hits dried up. She retired to raise her family, got out of the music business and fell on hard times, at one point becoming a bus driver to earn money. She later began acting on TV, in films and on Broadway, and in 1989 she won a Tony Award for her performance in *Black and Blue* on Broadway and won a Grammy in the category Best Jazz Performance for the album *Blues on Broadway*. She passed away in 2006.

3. "Tighten Up" | Archie Bell and the Drells (1968)

As some details in the write-up for "(There's Gonna Be A) Showdown" explained, Archie Bell first formed his group in 1966 and in 1967 recorded "Tighten Up" on the Texas-based Ovide label. With its lead-in that proudly proclaimed they were "Archie Bell and the Drells from Houston, Texas," sales took off in the South. "I said that about being from Texas because after the Kennedy assassination I heard a DJ say nothing good had ever come out of Texas," Bell told me. "I knew that wasn't true, and that was my way of making a statement." It certainly didn't hurt sales, as the record sold several hundred thousand copies regionally before coming to the attention of Atlantic records, which released it nationally and watched it sell a million records, climb all the way to #1 and earn a gold record in 1968. Bell was shocked, telling me, "We never thought 'Tighten Up' would be as big as it was, and it was a real surprise to everybody." Other than Bell's vocals, the other Drells didn't contribute much else other than hand clapping and whistling because the instrumental work was by a Texas group called the TSU Tornadoes.

Oddly enough, Bell first heard about the record's success from a hospital bed in Germany because he'd been drafted before the record went national:

I served in the Fifty-Third Transportation Unit stationed in Germany. I'd been in a wreck and was in the hospital when my manager called me and told me that "Tighten Up" has just gone gold. Earlier I'd been telling the guys I served with, "Hey, that music you hear on the radio, that's me." One of them said "You guys from Texas sure can tell some big lies! I guess that's because everything's big in Texas!" They didn't believe me. But when I rolled my wheelchair down the hall and told my buddies my record had gone gold, and they realized what I'd been telling them was really true—it really was me! Suddenly I had an entourage! We'd be on bivouac and there'd be twelve men trying to get in a four-man tent. Everywhere I went people knew me. There was a paper called The Overseas Weekly, *and about two weeks later they had an article there about me that said I was "the richest GI in the Army since Elvis!" It was really all a dream.*

Fortunately, the army was pretty liberal with Bell after "Tighten Up" became a hit and frequently allowed him to go home for a few days and perform. That story is continued in the write-up for "(There's Gonna Be A) Showdown."

4. "One Mint Julep" | The Clovers

This track was previously on Atlantic's *Beach Beat*. See that album for details about the song.

5. "Walking Up a One Way Street" | Willie Tee

This track was previously on Atlantic's *Beach Beat*. See that album for details about the song.

6. "I've Got Sand in My Shoes" | The Drifters (1964)

In 1964, the Drifters released "One Way Love," followed in June by "Under the Boardwalk" (the background on those records can be found earlier in this chapter). Their next release was "I've Got Sand in My Shoes," and once again, Johnny Moore sang lead vocals on the song. Like "Under the Boardwalk," the song was written by Arthur Resnick and Kenny Young.

As with "Under the Boardwalk," "Sand in My Shoes" is as much about the beach as a record can get, and in fact, Michael Jack Kirby of *Way Back Attack* said "the Drifters were thereafter strongly associated with the Carolina 'beach' music scene." It would be hard to disagree. The singer (in this case, Johnny Moore) sings about the time he spent with his girlfriend on the beach, recalling the boardwalk, the crowds, the heat, the salt air and, above all, the sand he still has in his shoes.

Nationally, the song didn't do quite as well as "Under the Boardwalk," however. It topped out at #33 on the pop charts and #21 on the R&B charts. Even though the Drifters had been producing hits for more than a decade, their next release, "Saturday Night at the Movies," would sadly be their last Top 20 pop hit in the United States. For more on their later career (the period during which they are often called the "English Drifters"), see the Ripete Beach Beat albums.

6

THE GAME CHANGER:
BEACH BEAT CLASSICS

RIPETE RECORDS 39146, 1980

*W*hile the chapter on *Ocean Drive Volume 1* preceded this chapter on Ripete Records' first *Beach Beat Classics* album, no one really seems to know which album came out first. Ed Weiss said, "They came out at about the same time," and Marion Carter concurred: "I think *Beach Beat* and Warner's *Ocean Drive* came out virtually the same week." It's like the chicken or the egg, but it doesn't really matter. What's clear is that two great and groundbreaking albums came out almost simultaneously in 1980 to break a long drought and change the availability of beach music forever. However, while the *Ocean Drive* albums were far less than successful, *Beach Beat Classics* were the first in a long string of quality albums that Ripete produced over the next forty years.

By 1980, despite all the trial and error that had taken place up to that point, the beach music compilation albums had been less than spectacular in terms of sales. What really saved the beach music compilation album business was Ripete Records.

Founded by Marion Carter and Pete Smolen—and named for them (Marion [Ri] and Pete [Pete]) as well—Ripete became the label to go to for any and all beach music and spawned countless imitators. How it came into existence is a story in itself.

"I started as a mobile DJ in the mid-'70s," Marion Carter told me, "playing fraternity parties, weddings, things like that. This was right when the disco era was kicking in, 1976 and '77, and punk rock was starting. But during my DJ engagements I was getting more requests for beach music than all other kinds of music combined, which was kind of shocking, honestly. I was a beach fan, and had friends who were in that circle, but I wasn't just thinking about it, but everywhere I'd go, people were asking me [to] 'play some beach music.'"

"It went on from there," he said.

I was playing a DJ party at a country club and had just played "39-21-40 Shape," and a guy walked up, pulled it off the turntable and threw down a twenty-dollar bill. He said, "I've been looking for this record and can't find it." I said, "Well, okay, I know where every record store is in South and North Carolina so I'll just get another copy." Well, so I went to Sumter to my favorite record store, and they were out of it. Went to Darlington Music, they didn't have it. I started thinking, "What's the deal here?" I tried five or six more stores, nobody had it. I thought "Oh my God, I shot one of my feet off here. That was one of my big call records and now I don't have it." I finally found a copy of "39-21-40 Shape" and bought it from a guy for ten dollars. It didn't mean as much to him as it did to me!

After that, I started asking about other records. Billy Stewart, "Fat Boy." "Nope," they'd say, "haven't had that in years." One thing after another. Everything was out of print. It was amazing. You couldn't buy any of them. This is when the light bulb came on. This stuff was out of print, and there was a groundswell in popularity for beach music. The record companies weren't even thinking about that old music anymore, and about the only thing you could buy even remotely related to beach music was like a Drifters Greatest Hits *album. Some things were just impossible to find.*

Carter said that in November 1979 he was in a new record store in Columbia that Pete Smolen had opened up called Sounds Familiar. When Smolen was a student at Duke, he worked in a Record Bar store near campus, and he went to work for them after college and worked his way up to head buyer when Record Bar had 180 stores and was one of the largest chains in the country. Eventually, he left Record Bar to open his own stores, first in Columbia, then Myrtle Beach, Asheville and a few other places. "Now Pete's store was different from other record stores," Carter said. "Where other stores would mainly carry oldies in the form of 'greatest hits' albums, he'd carry all the groups' LPs. I was in there one day buying albums, and so I went up front to check out. I'd been in four or five times and he knew my face, and about halfway through the stack he says, 'Who are you, and what do you do?' I said, 'Well, I've got a DJ business.' We talked more and I said, 'You know, I've been doing this DJ work, and people are driving me nuts about these beach songs.'" Smolen said, "Tell me more about this beach music. People come in asking me about it, but I don't know anything about it."

Carter recalled that at that point he'd been calling record labels to see if he could get a licensing deal done, but he'd had no luck.

> *I told him* [Smolen] *about beach music and what I had tried to do, and he said, "I know the president of Columbia/Epic records on a first-name basis." Now I'm thinking, "he doesn't know the president of Epic records," but I didn't know about his background then either. He starts telling me how he was the buyer at Record Bar and he'd played poker with the Columbia president and so on. He says, "Let me call Don Dempsey at Columbia." He gets him on the phone, and after they bs for about ten minutes he looks at me and says, "What songs are you looking for?" I rattled off five or six songs that I wanted to use that were out of print. When Smolen got off the phone he said that Dempsey had told him, "Yeah, I'm gonna clear those five songs, and I'll call Warner Brothers, Polygram, Motown and connect you guys up." I was nervous and shaking, I didn't really even know Pete, but at that point I said, "If you're willing, I'd like to form a partnership with you." We talked about it and shook hands right there, went out to eat, stayed out till three in the morning and came up with a game plan. All of sudden my dream had come true, and the fact that it lasted forty-plus years is something that's beyond amazing to me. We never had a cross word, and it was a partnership made in heaven. Few people get to do something for a living that is their hobby, but that's how it all started.*

(Unfortunately, Smolen died the week before I interviewed Marion Carter in August 2023.)

As for the way they selected the content, "We loaded the first album up on side one with local and regional bands. We had the Band of Oz and the Catalinas and Cannonball and the Swingin' Medallions because we felt like the bands would be more energized about selling and promoting them at their shows." On side 1, only "Ms. Grace" had been on a compilation album and that was the bootlegged *Billy Smith's Beach Party*. For side 2, they used old standards, and on that side every song except "Te-Ta-Te-Ta-Ta" and "Give Me Just a Little More Time" had previously been on a compilation album— but again, that didn't mean they were still available. "It was startling how much stuff was out of print. The record people would actually laugh when we would ask for some obscure R&B tune. They'd say, 'What in the heck are you gonna do with this?'"

"It took until May of 1980 to get the albums out," Carter said.

> *The pressing plants were backed up. We used Dixie Pressing out of Nashville. We kept waiting and waiting for the records, and finally called them and said, "We're going to drive out there to get the albums, if you can just press a few thousand copies." We rented a van and drove to Nashville. They ran us 5000 copies of* Beach Beat Volume 1, *so we loaded them up and brought them back ourselves. Pete had been running advertisements in his store for about two weeks announcing the album, and when they went into the store, there would be several lines of people three and four deep, and it surpassed any of the biggest sellers he'd ever had in the store. In two weeks, we had to get another shipment for places like Record Bar, and I also drove around to little stores to get them to carry them too. It sold 50,000 copies that summer. By November we came out with* Beach Beat Volume 2, *and it had basically the same sales figures. We ended up selling over 100,000 of each of them before we quit tracking.*

Carter said that although they hoped the album would sell, they really were surprised by how well it did:

> *I knew we'd hit a home run that fall when we went to a Clemson football game, and we parked at Tillman Hall and had to walk across campus to the stadium. You'd walk a bit and hear one of the songs playing. Another few minutes, you'd hear another. People were playing the eight tracks or cassettes, because the songs weren't available any other way. I thought "Holy Cow, this thing is blowing up." I'll never forget that. We were just incredulous. It was amazing.*

Songs from the *It Will Stand* Top 50 list that appeared on previously released albums were "Ms. Grace," "Thank You John," "39-21-40 Shape" and "Fat Boy." In addition, "Across the Street" had now appeared on *Atlantic's Beach Beat Vol. 2*, *Billy Smith's Beach Party*, *Ocean Drive Volume 1* and this album, making it unquestionably the most often-anthologized song at this point. Three songs from the *It Will Stand* Top 50 list appeared here for the first time on a licensed album: "Summertime's Calling Me," "39-21-40 Shape" and "A Quiet Place" (the latter two songs appeared on the unlicensed Billy Smith albums, however).

BEACH BEAT CLASSICS, 1980

Side A: New Waves
1. "Summertime's Calling Me," The Catalinas
2. "Ms. Grace," The Tymes
3. "Myrtle Beach Days," The Fantastic Shakers
4. "Shaggin'," The Band of Oz
5. "If I Didn't Have a Dime," Bob Collins and the Fabulous Five
6. "You Keep Telling Me Yes," Cannonball
7. "Would You Believe," The Tempests
8. "Hey, Hey Baby," The Swingin' Medallions

Side B: Old Waves
1. "39-21-40 Shape," The Showmen
2. "Thank You John," Willie Tee
3. "Fat Boy," Billy Stewart
4. "A Quiet Place," Garnet Mimms and the Enchanters.
5. "Across the Street," Lenny O'Henry
6. "I Got the Fever," The Georgia Prophets
7. "Te-Ta-Te-Ta-Ta," Ernie K. Doe
8. "Give Me Just a Little More Time," The Chairmen of the Board

The Songs

Side A: New Waves
1. "Summertime's Calling Me" | The Catalinas (1975)

Originally formed in 1958, the Catalinas became popular playing fraternity parties and dances in the Carolinas. They eventually graduated to playing the Myrtle Beach Pavilion, reportedly drawing the some of the largest crowds that venue ever saw. Early on, the group recorded occasionally on small labels but had no national hits. By 1967, the group was working with high school classmate Ted Hall and his booking agency Hit Attractions, and Hall arranged to have the group go to Nashville and record some songs, among them "You Haven't the Right." The song was released on the Scepter label, and although it did well in some regional markets, it didn't sell in large numbers nationally. The group recorded some other tracks for the label, but none were ever released, so the group carried on, its lineup ever-changing, still waiting for that hit that eluded them. They changed their sound at one point to mirror some of the popular horn bands in the late 1960s and early '70s, but by about 1973 they had moved back to beach music.

In 1972, Johnny Barker, the group's keyboardist, wrote "Summertime's Calling Me" one night on the way to Boone, North Carolina, to play a gig. "I was trying to come up with an idea for a song," Barker told the author.

Two lines—"I want to sit there in the sand," "and watch those golden tans go walking by"—came to me. After trying for a while to come up with something that everyone could relate to, especially the college crowds, I came up with "I know it isn't fair, cause you might really care, but it's different now, that summertime's calling me." I mean, after all, we all can't wait for the end of winter's misery and that first real summer vacation, and so I thought I had what we in the music business call a good "hook" for a song at the very least. Well, I was driving alone, but knew for certain I had to write this down. So I found a matchbook cover in the car and carefully scribbled the chorus down. I knew the rest of the story would come in time.

When the song was completed, the group recorded it and added it to their repertoire, but much to their disappointment, it didn't catch on at first. Bandmember Gary Barker noted, "We were really excited about it and started performing it everywhere we went, but nothing happened and nobody seemed interested. Finally, we even kinda quit playing it."

"And then something very strange happened during one of our jobs at a sorority party at Wofford College," Johnny Barker said.

We introduced "Summertime's Calling Me" as our latest recording and stood there amazed at what we saw next. All of the girls in the sorority lined up and performed for us while we played. Not only did they know all of the words to our song, but they had their own version of a line dance they had created for each line of the song. I remember Gary and I looking at each other in disbelief at what was going on. From that night forward, "Summertime's Calling Me" grew quickly in popularity, mainly on college campuses in Georgia and the Carolinas. It became an anthem for getting out of town, heading for the beach and, most of all, for having fun.

"Summertime's Calling Me" has since come to be regarded as the first "new" beach song, as it predated other now-classic regional beach hits such as "I Love Beach Music," "Myrtle Beach Days" and "Carolina Girls." "Summertime's" started a new trend: the composition and marketing of songs about the beach *designed* to be beach music. Within a few years, bands all over the South were recording songs about beach music itself, about sitting on the beach, about summertime and any and all associated areas of beach music. Though the Catalinas have had a frequently changing roster over the last fifty-plus years, their legacy will always be as the group that recorded   "Summertime's Calling Me" and thus started the emergence of original beach music that continues to this day.

2. "Ms. Grace" | The Tymes

This is a repeated track from *Billy Smith's Beach Party.* See that album for details about the song.

3. "Myrtle Beach Days" | The Fantastic Shakers (1978)

North Carolina native Jeffrey Lynn Reid began his career as a professional musician when he joined the house band at the Shadow Club in Newton, North Carolina, and by 1975, he was working in Myrtle Beach playing an after-hours bar called the Army-Navy Club. "I was twenty years old and played from midnight to five in the morning," Reid told me. "A lot of groups would come in after they finished at the clubs where they were playing, and sometimes they'd jam with us." One person who came into the club was Bo Schronce of the Catalinas, who sang lead on "Summertime's Calling Me." Reid got to know Schronce and eventually played him an original composition called "Myrtle Beach Days," based, oddly enough, on the Queen song called "Killer Queen." "It originally sounded a lot like 'Killer Queen' in fact, with the piano—well actually, it didn't sound *that* good!" Reid said. Reid and his song made an impression on Schronce, and when he left

the Catalinas to form a new band in late 1977, Schronce asked Reid to join the group and he agreed. The new group eventually decided to become "a beach and R&B band," Reid said. "Bo wanted to do Las Vegas–style shows. He saw a group called the Fantastic Puzzle who did floor shows, and there was also a local band called the Shakers who used to perform. He just put the two names together to come up with the Fantastic Shakers."

Just as the Catalinas had jumped to the forefront of the beach music scene with Johnny Barker's "Summertime's Calling Me," Schronce knew better than anyone that the Shakers needed their own signature song. That's where "Myrtle Beach Days" came in. "Bo said, 'We ought to take that old song of yours, "Myrtle Beach Days," and make it a beach song'" Reid says. Despite the fact that it was modeled after a '70s rock song, Reid says the conversion wasn't all that difficult. With Schronce's distinctive voice singing lead, the song was a hit. "By 1980, when our album came out, it was really big," Reid said. "I remember playing in Columbia in 1980 at the stadium and there were six to eight thousand people there. It was quite a time."

Reid stayed with the Shakers until 1994, when he decided to go out his own again, filling in with different bands from time to time and recording as well. "When I play solo, I still get asked to play 'Myrtle Beach Days' a lot. I'm glad it made the impression it made on so many people."

4. "Shaggin'" | The Band of Oz (1978)

The group got their start in the late 1960s as the Avengers, but by 1970, they had changed their name to the Band of Oz, added horns and expanded their playlist as they played the party and club circuit. They performed across the South, but after "playing full-time traveling all over the Southeast" for several years but "tired of being on the road," member Keith Houston said the group decided to go back to their roots and specialize by playing what was known in the Carolinas as beach music. "We figured...we could go back to North Carolina and do that type of music again, so we came back home started playing the old beach music that we used to play. It was actually getting big then, and new beach music was being written as well."

That "new" beach music had become extremely popular, and the Band of Oz decided to offer up their own contribution in the form of "Shaggin'" in 1978. "Billy Bazemore was our lead vocalist, and he came in one day and said 'Look, I gotta set of lyrics here, I've written a song,'" Houston told me. "Well, he pulls out *four pages* of lyrics—it was probably three or four songs! I took it and edited down and put the music to it. And though we had two or three songs worth of lyrics, we did get one real good hit out of it." They tested it out by playing it in their act, and after "playing it live before we ever made the record...we decided to record it. It was the first time our band had actually been in the studio." The band went to Mega Sound in North Carolina and recorded the song with Bazemore singing lead. "You never know what's going to happen when you make a record," Houston said, "but we got a good response. We started pushing it at the radio stations. All the beach jocks started to play it, and it got a lot of airplay. Then when Ripete Records came in and put together that first *Beach Beat* album, and it had 'Shaggin'' on it along with 'Myrtle Beach Days,' 'I Love Beach Music" and also a lot of national releases, it locked it in as a beach music hit."

In 1982, another big hit came along—actually one that was even bigger—when they recorded "Ocean Boulevard," which went on to win song of the year at the Carolina Beach Music Awards. "We don't play 'Shaggin' all that much now. Even though it was one of the biggest selling things we did, we only play it once in a great while. But you know, I think it's one of those things that if we did it every night, we'd be indoctrinating another group of kids, because most people are more familiar with the newer stuff. But they are still great songs."

5. "If I Didn't Have a Dime" | Bob Collins and the Fabulous Five (1966)

Donny Trexler formed his first band, Donny and the Blue Jets, when he was fourteen, and eventually, they morphed into Bob Collins and the Fabulous Five by 1962 (see chapter 4 on "Inventory on Heartaches"). In 1964, the group heard a song called "If I Didn't Have a Dime" by the Los Angeles–based Furys. "If I Didn't Have a Dime" was written by Bert Russell and Phil Medley, who also wrote songs such as "Twist and Shout" and "A Million to One," and it had first appeared as the flipside of Gene Pitney's 1962 smash "Only Love Can Break a Heart." The Furys single hadn't sold well, but apparently their cover made enough of an impression that the group decided incorporate the song into their act. "We put it together, and the college kids really loved it," Trexler told me. "We played a lot of fraternity parties, and they always wanted to hear it. The song was so popular that we went to Arthur Smith Studios and recorded it in late 1964, but we didn't like the recording. But we'd been playing it live and people were going crazy for it, so finally we re-recorded it late in the summer of 1966 at Copeland Sound Studios." In order to bring the energy and enthusiasm that accompanied those live performances at clubs and fraternity parties across the South, "we took the recording to a club in Greensboro called the Jokers Three. We played the song and acted like we were singing it, and we got the people to carry on and we recorded the audience and the background noise. What you hear there on the song is exactly what we heard and what it sounded like when we played it at parties and in clubs. People went crazy over

it. The fans were great, and we wanted the recording to sound the way they liked the song to sound."

Although the single sold only regionally, the song's popularity contributed to the group's renown and led to them playing with the Four Tops, Martha and the Vandellas, Major Lance and many other acts, some of the biggest names of the decade. The Fabulous Five's next release was a song Trexler had written called "Inventory on Heartaches." They recorded it with Collins on lead and Trexler playing guitar and singing backup while arranging the song as well.

Eventually, Trexler left the group, having decided "it was time to move on." Bob Collins and the Fabulous Five disbanded not long after Trexler left, while Trexler joined the O'Kaysions for a while, formed a band called Swing from 1972 until 1986 and then began performing with his wife, Susan. Trexler, who still owns the rights to the name Bob Collins and the Fabulous Five and their recordings, won a CAMMY Award for "Lifetime Achievement" in November 2000 and was inducted into the South Carolina Rhythm and Blues Hall of Fame, among other accolades.

6. "You Keep Telling Me Yes" | Cannonball (1973)

In the mid-1960s, Joe Clinard was a member of Calvin Lindsay and the Hysterics, a regional band from High Point, North Carolina. The group was popular on the beach club circuit and recorded some cover songs on the Greensboro-based Jokers 3 label around 1966. Clinard left the group in 1967 for basic training and then joined the Impacts; the band later became

Flagstone and soon changed their name once again and became Cannonball. Clinard said they changed the name because he felt they needed to in order to get some airplay, and as they were becoming a bit more of a beach music band they needed to forge a new identity. Clinard soon became the band's manager, and the group often played at a bar over the Idle Hour Arcade near the Pavilion in Myrtle Beach, which eventually became the

Castaways. Clinard said they played there with bands such as "the Showmen, Dr. Hook and Nantucket, to name a few." In 1973, the group recorded their second single, the beach music classic "You Keep Telling Me Yes," at Reflection Sound Studios in Charlotte. On that song, the group worked with producer Duke Hall, who had also produced the Platters' hits "With This Ring," "Washed Ashore" and "I Love You 1,000 Times." Clinard said, "Hall not only produced the song, he also did horns and strings."

Released on the group's own Blast label, the song was instantly popular on the beach music circuit, selling thousands of copies. Unfortunately, as is the case with many regional hits, that didn't translate to national sales, so the success of the group's big moment was confined principally to the Carolinas. However, a measure of the song's enduring popularity was that the single was so much in demand that bootlegs started to come out—which is almost unheard of for a regional release. "Blast was our label," Clinard said, "but then the record showed up on the Reflection label, and then Shadow. As is often the case, I'm not sure what happened to the royalties from sales through the years, because I only saw some in the early '70s."

Despite the record's solid sound, the group's makeup changed very quickly, and though Clinard tried to hold the group together, it was becoming more and more of a problem. "I was trying to sing songs that I hadn't sung lead on originally, and I didn't feel good doing that. I think we were booked on a show with Cornelius Brothers and Sister Rose and about the third day of the gig I called the guys together backstage and told them 'I can't do this anymore.' I never did walk on a stage again." Clinard left the music business, became a successful businessman and founded a number of enterprises, including Cheap Joe's, Texas Jeans and AQUA Boutiques.

7. "Would You Believe" | The Tempests (1967)

The Tempests originated in Charlotte, North Carolina, in the early 1960s when high school student John Branch founded a cover band called the Larks; he later changed the group's name to the Tempests after reading *The Tempest* by William Shakespeare. They worked as a backup band most of the time, but they heard about a singer named Hazel Walker who sang with the Pastels and decided to invite him to join. Through a series of mix-ups, they ended up finding singer Hazel *Martin* instead, who became the group's lead during their most productive period. They cut some demos and eventually got a recording deal with the Smash label, which had also signed the Swingin' Medallions and for whom the Georgia Prophets recorded "I Got the Fever."

The group was still playing fraternity parties and clubs in the South when their first single for Smash, the 1967 classic "Would You Believe," was released. While the song performed well in the Southeast, it made little impact west of the Mississippi and did not break into the Hot 100, though it did manage to "bubble under" on the national charts at #127. Smash followed up with an album of the same name, but their next two singles failed to chart. The group was touring extensively during this period and found themselves on the bill with acts such as the Four Tops and Jay and the Techniques.

As with many groups, with success came personnel problems, and eventually Martin left. From that point, the group's composition changed frequently. They recorded a few more singles before breaking up in 1975. Member Mike Branch went on to form Surfside Records in 1979 with General Johnson, and the label was home to "new" beach music hits by the Chairmen of the Board, the Poor Souls, the Band of Oz and others.

8. "Hey, Hey, Baby" | The Swingin' Medallions (1968)

For background on the group's early years and prior recording history, see the entry for "Double Shot" on *Billy Smith's Beach Party Volume 2* (chapter 4).

After the group's million-seller "Double Shot (of My Baby's Love)" on the Smash label, the group next released "She Drives Me Out of My Mind." John McElrath told me it intentionally sounded a lot like "Double Shot" but was nowhere near as successful, topping out at #71 on the pop charts. It was clear their niche was performing as a "party band"—a title they happily embrace to this day—as one song after another was released to capitalize on that reputation. They moved to Capitol records, and their next release was another party track, a version of Bruce Channel's "Hey! Baby" called "Hey, Hey, Baby." Channel had recorded it in 1961, and after it became a regional hit, Smash Records picked it up for national distribution and it went to #1 on the pop charts. The Medallions' version is mainly a speeded-up horn version more appropriate for a party atmosphere than Channel's slower cut. In any event, the Medallions' version did not chart but has become a southern party staple nonetheless.

Eventually, band members went their separate ways, some going on to form the group Pieces of Eight, most going back to college to finish their educations. "We had a lot of fun," McElrath told me. "I think we just lucked into it." The band and their music have become legendary in the Carolinas, and though John McElrath passed away, his sons carry on his legacy. They play "Hey, Hey, Baby" to this day.

Side B: Old Waves
1. "39-21-46" | The Showmen

(Note: "39-21-46" is the song title as it appears on the album). This track was previously on *Billy Smith's Beach Party*. See that album for details about the song.

2. "Thank You John" | Willie Tee

This track was previously on Atlantic's *Beach Beat*. See that album for details about the song.

3. "Fat Boy" | Billy Stewart

This track was previously on Atlantic's *Beach Beat Vol 2*. See that album for details about the song.

4. "A Quiet Place" | Garnet Mimms and the Enchanters

This track was previously on *Billy Smith's Beach Party Volume 2*. See that album for details about the song.

5. "Across the Street" | Lenny O'Henry

This track was previously on Atlantic's *Beach Beat Vol 2*. See that album for details about the song.

6. "I Got the Fever" | The Georgia Prophets

This track was previously on *Billy Smith's Beach Party Volume 2*. See that album for details about the song.

7. "Te-Ta-Te-Ta-Ta" | Ernie K. Doe (1961)

Born Ernest Kador Jr. in New Orleans, as a teenager he started singing in nightclubs. In 1954, he joined a group called the Blue Diamonds, and they recorded one single for Savoy. Eventually, he had the opportunity to record a few solo sides, and he released one as Ernest Kador on Specialty and another as Ernie Kado and yet another as Ernie K. Doe on Ember. In 1959, he signed with Minit, where he had the chance to work for the now-legendary Allen Toussaint. His first single didn't do anything, though the next, 1960's "Hello Lover," generated enough regional interest that it reportedly sold 100,000 copies. His next release was the 1961 smash "Mother-in-Law."

"Mother-in-Law," written by Toussaint, was a playful tune in the vein of many of the Coasters hits. One thing that really made the song work was the contribution of backup Benny Spellman, who at the time was also a struggling artist for Minit. Spellman agreed to help out on "Mother-in-Law," and his bass voice can be heard echoing K. Doe by singing the words "mother-in-law" throughout the record. The song went to #1 on the pop and the R&B charts.

At the next recording session to follow up "Mother-in-Law," K. Doe recorded "'Get Out of My House" and "Te-Ta-Te-Ta-Ta." Though 1961's "Te-Ta-Te-Ta-Ta" wasn't a big hit, over time it has come to be regarded as a beach music classic. "That was written because Ernie had his trademark style of singing where he'd go 'ah-ah-ah,'" Deacon John Moore, a session musician who played on the song, told me. "And so Allen wrote 'Te-Ta-Te-Ta-Ta' to rhyme with that." "Te-Ta-Te-Ta-Ta" went to #53 on the Top 100 and #21 on the R&B charts.

K. Doe had a number of releases over the years that would chart out of the Top 40, but eventually he opted for a career in radio in the 1980s. K. Doe opened the Mother-in-Law Lounge in New Orleans in 1994 and frequently performed there, often in a cape and a crown in his "Emperor of the Universe" persona. A flamboyant performer until the end, he died from liver and kidney failure in 2001.

8. "Give Me Just a Little More Time" | The Chairmen of the Board (1970)

General Norman Johnson started as a member of Humdingers, a group that eventually became the Showmen and signed with Minit records (for background on the Showmen, see the entry on *Billy Smith's Beach Party*

Volume 2). He left that group in 1968 and formed the Chairmen of the Board with Danny Woods, Harrison Kennedy and Eddie Curtis. They were to work for the famed songwriting team of Brian Holland, Lamont Dozier and Eddie Holland—generally referred to as Holland-Dozier-Holland—who by that time had left Motown to form their own Invictus label. The Chairmen's "Give Me Just a Little More Time" was just the fourth release by the new label and launched Invictus in a spectacular fashion.

"Give Me Just a Little More Time" had instrumental backing by the famous Funk Brothers of Motown, who often moonlighted on labels to supplement their notoriously low Motown salaries. The song was written by Holland-Dozier-Holland of course, but that's not what the label says. When Holland-Dozier-Holland left Motown acrimoniously, they were sued for breach of contract, and for years they were unable to put their real names on the songs they wrote. In the case of "Give Me Just a Little More Time," which they wrote with associate Ron Dunbar, the label credits say it was written by "Edythe Wayne" and Ron Dunbar (Edith Wayne was the name of a family friend).

The song went all the way to #3 on the pop charts and to #2 in England. The record sold more than one million copies, and the group was awarded a gold record by the Recording Industry Association of America. The group went on to have three more Top 40 hits in rapid succession, and "You've Got Me Dangling on a String"(Pop #38), "Everything's Tuesday" (Pop #38) and "Pay to the Piper"(Pop #13) became beach music hits in time. In the meantime, Johnson was writing hits for other artists as well. He wrote "Patches," which Clarence Carter recorded in 1970 and which won Johnson a Grammy award and contributed to his distinction of being named BMI songwriter of the year; "Bring the Boys Home" for Freda Payne; the million-seller "Somebody's Been Sleeping" for 100 Proof Aged in Soul; and the #1 million seller "Want Ads" for Honey Cone.

Unfortunately, Johnson and Invictus weren't seeing eye to eye on monetary matters. Johnson left the label for a career as a solo act, but he soon re-formed the Chairmen of the Board with former original member Danny Woods and former backup member Ken Knox. After two decades of singing for different labels, Virginia-born Johnson decided it was time to go home. Knox told me that Johnson told him and Woods, "'We're gonna go down to the Carolinas and do this music they have called beach music. I'm going to write some songs about the culture, where all the kids go down to the beach and places like the Pad." In 1979, Johnson and Mike Branch (formerly of the Tempests) formed Surfside Records, and a whole new era began for the group. Kicked off by 1980's "On the Beach," they followed with now-classics such as "Carolina Girls," "Down at the Beach Club" and others. As Johnson himself later said, "For the first time in eight years, I enjoyed performing music without the depression of the music business. I found an independent music industry that was still free of monopoly, politics and categorization." The band became *the* face of Carolina beach music and recorded some of the genre's greatest hits of all time.

Johnson passed away in 2010, and Danny Woods passed away in 2018. Ken Knox still performs to this day.

7

THE RISE OF THE BEACH MUSIC COMPILATION ALBUM ON VINYL, 1981-82

*A*s 1981 began, there had been one Warner's *Ocean Drive* album and one Ripete *Beach Beat* album released in 1980. The next year saw the release of two more of Warner's *Ocean Drive* albums, while Ripete released two more *Beach Beat* albums as well as *Shagger's Delight*, an album made up of previously unavailable Federal and King releases. In 1982, Ripete released a fourth *Beach Beat* album, and CBS/Epic Records, Surfside Records and Arista also released beach music compilation albums, bringing the total to nine new beach music albums in a two-year period—this as opposed to five legally licensed albums *total* released in the fourteen years (inclusive) from 1967 to 1980. Clearly, something was going right, and it was obvious that five record companies were paying licensing costs to produce a product for a market that was obviously growing.

Because an in-depth discussion about each of these albums as in previous chapters would more than double the size of this work, brief overviews of the albums released in 1981 and 1982 follow. The following albums are in alphabetical order by title.

BEACH BEAT CLASSICS VOLUME II
(RIPETE RECORDS 15693, 1981)

Four songs previously unreleased on a beach compilation album from the *It Will Stand* list were on this album, those being the Trammps' "Hold Back the Night," the Chairmen of the Board's "Everything's Tuesday," the Platters' "With This Ring" and Jimmy Ricks and the Ravens' "Green Eyes." Maurice Williams and the Zodiacs' "May I" was on Atlantic's *Beach Beat Vol. 2* and the Globetrotters' "Rainy Day Bells" appeared on the first bootleg Billy Smith album. That being said, what was and wasn't on previous albums was beside the point—this was an exceptional album. In addition to the four first-time releases from the *It Will Stand* list, the Drifters' "(You're More than a Number in) My Little Red Book" and "Kissin' in the Back Row" were relatively new songs, having been released during the "English" phase of the Drifters' career in the 1970s. These songs were already well on their way to becoming classics, and the same can be said for Jerry Butler's "Cooling Out." The Futures' "Party Time Man" and Jim Gilstrap's "Swing Your Daddy" were also great songs, very big in the '70s, and all-around solid entries. On side 2, the Benny Spellman classic "Lipstick Traces" was a song that was not, but should have been, on the *It Will Stand* Top 50 list, and the same could be said for The O'Jays' "I Dig Your Act." Rounding out the list were the O'Jays' "Lonely Drifter," the Tams' "Too Much Fooling Around" and the Intruders' "Cowboys to Girls." So all in all this was an exceptional album.

BEACH BEAT CLASSICS VOLUME III
(RIPETE RECORDS 392148, 1981)

Two previously unreleased songs from the *It Will Stand* list were on this album, the Embers' "I Love Beach Music" and the Chairmen of the Board's "(You've Got Me) Dangling on a String." Though the first of these has been played so often that many beach music aficionados now find this "beach music about beach music" song to be tiresome, you have to remember it was an important song, especially in 1981. However, the other songs on side 1 were very much a mixed bag. The Love Committee's "Cheaters Never Win" and the Drifters' "Do You Have to Go Now" were both good '70s cuts, and Dale Van Horn's "That's Summertime to Me" and Clifford Curry's "Shag with Me" were so-so. It's quite hard to understand the selection of the Poor Souls' version of the Coasters' "Brazil" over the original, other than the fact that Atlantic/Atco owned the right to the original versions of the song and Atlantic/Atco titles were being sold to the *Ocean Drive* compilers at that time. Side 2 did contain two songs that had been on *Summer Souvenirs* in 1969, Clifford Curry's classic "We're Gonna Hate Ourselves in the Morning" and the Zodiacs' "Stay." Other good songs on side 2 were Roscoe Gordon's "Surely I Love You," Wilbert Harrison's "Don't Drop It," Jewell and the Rubies' "Kidnapper," the Intrigues' "In a Moment," Louis Prima & Keely Smith's "Just a Gigolo" and the Tams' "Laugh It Off" and "You Lied to Your Daddy." You could make a case that every one of these side 2 selections could have made the *It Will Stand* list, and had the list gone to one hundred, it would be hard to see how they could be excluded.

There were two outliers on the album, side 1's inclusion of the Fantastic Shakers doing a cover of the Rascals' "It's a Beautiful Morning," originally a flower power era soft-rock tune, and on side 2, "Elvira," a country song by Dallas Frazier. This was the first notable instance of what would be an all-too-common occurrence in the coming years: compiling songs that could be shagged to under the umbrella of beach music. In 1979, General Johnson recognized

that the thriving beach music market "was slowly being recognized as too dependent on old recordings," which eventually led to the inclusion of shagable songs that weren't truly beach music making their way onto compilation albums. By the time Ripete's *Beach Beat Classics Volume V* was released in 1988, arguably only one selection of the fourteen songs on the album—Wild Cherry's "1 2 3 Kind of Love"—would have been called "beach music" back in 1981, and that was by the thinnest of margins. Sadly, the inclusion of these two songs on this album was perhaps the first indication that "times were a-changing," as they say.

OCEAN DRIVE VOLUME II
(WARNER SPECIAL PRODUCTS 2525, 1981)

Volume II was another big four-sided set of beach classics, and this time the album didn't almost exclusively feature Atlantic/Atco selections. Liberty, MCA, Double Shot, Brunswick and other labels were represented, and by doing so a number of songs from the *It Will Stand* list were compiled for the first time. The #1 song on their list, Billy Ward & the Dominoes' "Sixty Minute Man," was included here, marking its first time on a licensed album, as were the Platters' "Washed Ashore," the Embers' "Far Away Places," the Tams' "Be Young, Be Foolish, Be Happy," Bruce Channel's "Hey! Baby," the Showmen's "It Will Stand" and Deon Jackson's "Love Makes the World Go Round." Previously compiled classics "A Quiet Place" and "Rainy Day Bells" were also included, as was "Girl Watcher," which had previously appeared only on the first Billy Smith bootleg album.

The album included top-tier beach classics such as the Tams' "Silly Little Girl," Leon Haywood's "It's Got to Be Mellow," the Astors' "Candy," Brenton Wood's "Gimme Little Sign," Darrell Banks' "Open the Door to Your Heart," J.J. Jackson's "But It's Alright," Arthur Alexander's

"Anna" and Jackie Wilson's "Whispers." Solid efforts such as the Drifters' "Come on Over to My Place" and "At the Club," Jackie Moore's "Both Ends Against the Middle," Archie Bell and the Drells' "Girl, You're Too Young," Willie Tee's "You Better Say Yes" and the Swingin' Medallions' "She Drives Me Out of My Mind" rounded out the album. Like the first *Ocean Drive* album, it compiled exceptional selections without plugging in marginal tracks.

OCEAN DRIVE VOLUME III
(WARNER SPECIAL PRODUCTS 2526, 1981)

Included songs from the *It Will Stand* list previously unreleased on a beach compilation album were the Tams' "I've Been Hurt," the Artistics' "I'm Gonna Miss You," Jackie Wilson's "Higher and Higher," and Archie Bell and the Drells' "I Can't Stop Dancing." Remarkably, this was the first album to feature songs licensed by Motown and its subsidiaries, and from the *It Will Stand* list the Temptations' "My Girl," Marvin Gaye's "Stubborn Kind of Fellow" and Mary Wells's "My Guy" were included. First-time classic selections including Joe Turner's "Wee Baby Blues," Bill Deal and the Rhondels' "What Kind of Fool Do You Think I Am," the Impressions' "It's All Right," Judy Clay and William Bell's "Private Number," Patty & the Emblems' "Mixed Up, Shook Up Girl" and Edwin Starr's "(S.O.S.) Stop Her On Sight" were present, and other venerated beach tunes were

Robert John's "You Don't Need a Gypsy," the Elgins' "Heaven Must Have Sent You," James and Bobby Purify's "Let Love Come Between Us." As expected from an Atlantic partner company, two Drifters tunes, "There Goes My First Love" and "I'll Take You Where The Music's Playing," as well as the Atlantic/ Atco-owned original the Ripete album should have licensed, the Coasters' "Brazil." Finally, it included a relatively new song that was making inroads toward becoming a classic, Dionne Warwick's 1977 single "Do You Believe in Love at First Sight." Three songs—the Intrigues' "In a Moment," the Chairmen of the Board's "(You've Got Me) Dangling on a String" and the Zodiacs' "Stay"—had already appeared on compilation albums.

After the three *Ocean Drive* albums were released, they were repackaged and rereleased with new covers and sold on television—again. One was a two-album set and included what was supposed to be most of the best songs already on the first three albums, and the other was a three-album set, which had many of the previous releases reordered with a handful of new additions. From Motown there was Junior Walker & the All Stars' "What Does It Take (To Win Your Love)," Mary Wells's "The One Who Really Loves You," the Four Tops' "Baby I Need Your Loving" and the Isley Brothers "This Old Heart of Mine (Is Weak for You)," and non-Motown cuts were by Major Lance ("Um, Um, Um, Um, Um, Um") and Bill Deal and the Rhondels ("I've Been Hurt"). By this point, the *Ocean Drive* albums had become a confusing mess, and no doubt buyers who thought they were getting a new product were shocked to see that while what was here was good, there was very little new at all.

SHAGGER'S DELIGHT (RIPETE RECORDS 628, 1981)

"We decided to reserve the *Beach Beat Classics* albums for most of the '60s-type beach music and put the old '40s and '50s songs on another series," Marion Carter told me. Thus was born *Shagger's Delight*, which relied solely on classic tracks from King and Federal labels. The album contained old standards still well known and others perhaps a little more obscure by 1981. But familiar or not, Carter and Smolen went out of their way to get these titles. "We drove to Nashville met with the King-Federal guys. They'd put out a couple of reissue albums, but they weren't really beach titles." But Carter and Smolen knew there was a market for "the hard shag kind of stuff on *Shagger's Delight*."

The liner notes for this album say it all. They lead off with "You should have been there," and go on to explain "Maybe we can't be back at OD in 1951 shaggin' the night away, but...For those of you who were fortunate enough to experience those golden days of rhythm and blues in the late 40s, the 50s, and the early 60s...this album will be a good fundamental

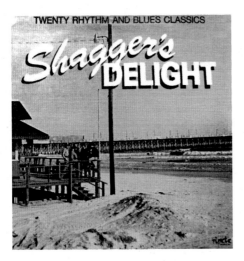

lesson in what true traditional beach music is all about." Included songs from the *It Will Stand* list previously unreleased on beach compilation albums were the Checkers' "White Cliffs of Dover," Wynonie Harris's "Good Rockin' Tonight" and the Five Royales' "Think," as well as "Sixty Minute Man" by the Dominoes, "one of the biggest most important songs in the history of music and massively popular," Carter said. "That song was the anchor on *Shagger's Delight*." While that song was on *Ocean Drive Volume II* as well, it's another "chicken or the egg" question in regard to which was first.

Other Dominoes tracks included "Pedal Pushing Pappa," the follow-up to "Sixty Minute Man" called "Can't Do Sixty No More," "Learning the Blues" and the excellent "Give Me You" from the period when Jackie Wilson was the group's lead singer. The Checkers' "Over the Rainbow," the Kingpins' "It Won't Be This Way Always" and the Lamplighters "I Used to Cry Mercy, Mercy" are songs that have a high standing in beach music circles even today. Instrumentals such as the three Earl Bostic selections have not aged as well, but Carter said, "Earl Bostic had been a big shag artist in the '40s and '50s," and so in keeping with the spirit of the album Bostic and Bill Doggett were included. The Five Royales' "Monkey Hips and Rice," the Platters' atypical "Beer Barrel Boogie" and "Stick" McGhee's usual raucous drinking songs "Jungle Juice," "Whiskey, Women and Loaded Dice" and "Six to Eight" are all good shag songs but not well known as beach songs. That being said, the album is true to what it says it will do and brings back those old classics no doubt many people had forgotten about, songs that were instrumental in the development of shagging.

1982

It was at this point, in 1982, where things started to get strange on some levels. Ripete released *Beach Beat Volume IV*, which would be the last album in that series for about five years. It contained one song from the *It Will Stand* list, The Four Tops' "I Just Can't Get You Out of My Mind," and it went downhill from there. There were decent '70s-era songs by Carrie Lucas, the Drifters, the Fantastics, Billy Ocean, William Bell and Janice, as well as a "rediscovered" early James Brown cut from 1959, but nevertheless it wasn't up to the standards of the previous *Beach Beat Classics* albums. The Lamont Dozier track "Cool Mc Out," though good, was actually only about a year old, the Johnny Mathis track (yep, Johnny Mathis!) was also recent, as were the Lou Rawls and Archie Bell cuts and the Rockin Louie & the Mamma Jammers track—a group that was still wet behind the ears, so to speak. It was this latter group that suggested that Ripete was running out of good licensed beach hits to anthologize and filling the gaps with middling R&B tracks that could be shagged to. It would be hard to say the songs by Mathis, Rawls, the Drells and Rockin Louie were really beach music. Shag music maybe, but not beach music.

It's not like anyone else was doing any better, however. That year, CBS/Epic records released *Endless Beach*, and other than Robert John's "If You Don't Want My Love," in many cases the group name was right but the song was wrong. Major Lance, the Tymes and Tyrone Davis were big names, but the songs were, again, R&B but not necessarily beach music. Tower of Power's "You Ought to Be Havin' Fun" is a great party song though, and Spiral Starecase's "She's Ready" and Wild Cherry's "1 2 3 Kind of Love" are pretty good second-tier beach songs. The remaining songs, by the likes of the Spellbinders, Otis Leavill, Billy Butler and others, were neither big names nor were the songs anything special. This was clearly an album put together utilizing rights to songs under the CBS/Epic umbrella and pretty much nothing more. It was an attempted cash grab at best.

Arista's 1982 release *The Beat of the Beach* was certainly better than the CBS/Epic album, with about half of the songs being good tracks. No one would argue with the inclusion of Clifford Curry's "She Shot a Hole in My Soul," Don Gardner and Dee Dee Ford's "I Need Your Lovin'," Wilbert Harrison's "Don't Drop It," the Drifters' "Kissin' in the Back Row," James and Bobby Purify's "I'm Your Puppet," Patty & the

Emblems' "Mixed Up, Shook-Up Girl," the O'Jays' "I Dig Your Act" or the Trammps' "Hold Back the Night" on any album. The Delfonics' "La La Means I Love You," James and Bobby Purify's "Let Love Come Between Us" and the Van Dykes' "You're Shakin' Me Up" are good second-level beach songs, as is the obligatory Drifters song "There Goes My First Love." The other songs are either lesser songs by beach music artists (the Showmen, Clifford Curry, Garnet Mimms, General Johnson) or just filler by well-known R&B artists.

The final album that year was by General Johnson's Surfside Records, called simply *Beach Classics*. Due to Johnson's having been a member of the

Showmen, the album included the classics "39-21-40 Shape" and "It Will Stand," both of which had been on the original *It Will Stand* list. It also included newer songs by the Chairmen of the Board, "Beach Fever" and "Carolina Girls." There was a newer Tempests cut, a couple of unimpressive Poor Souls covers and a couple of so-so Band of Oz cuts, although a third, "Ocean Boulevard," is certainly in the category of "Summertime's

Calling Me" and "I Love Beach Music" in the sense that it's a good tune for a regionally produced song. Frankly, given the resources available to Surfside Records compared to labels such as Arista and CBS and Ripete's miss on Volume IV, it was an impressive accomplishment.

8

UNCOLLECTED CLASSICS AND THE DECLINE OF BEACH MUSIC ON VINYL

*A*s 1982 came to a close, just six songs on the *It Will Stand* list of the greatest beach hits had yet to be anthologized for the beach music market: Billy Stewart's "I Do Love You" and "Sitting in the Park," the Platters' "I Love You 1,000 Times," the Georgia Prophets' "California," the Radiants' "It Ain't No Big Thing" and Hank Ballard and the Midnighters' "Work with Me Annie." Songs by all of these artists except the Radiants and the Midnighters had been on prior beach music compilation albums, and especially given that it's often said that the Radiants' "It Ain't No Big Thing" is one of the most often performed live beach songs, it's puzzling it hadn't been collected yet. But it wasn't just classic songs from the *It Will Stand* list that were still un-anthologized. Gene Barbour and the Cavaliers' "I Need You," Eddie Holland's "Jamie," Spiral Starecase's "More Today than Yesterday," the Monzas "Hey, I Know You," Jimmy Ruffin's "What Becomes of the Brokenhearted," the Poets' "She Blew a Good Thing," Sunny & Phyllis's "If We Had to Do It All Over" and a wide array of songs by the Four Tops, the Georgia Prophets, Jerry Butler and the early Spinners were uncollected as of 1982. They'd all make it to beach music compilation albums eventually, but those "albums" were not the vinyl issues that fans of the genre had come to know and love.

Everything was about to change. The first compact disc was introduced in 1982, and as great as vinyl sounded (and has since become apparent, it *really* sounded good), storage, durability issues and the fact that you couldn't play an LP in your car all put the album on the endangered list once compact discs hit the streets en masse. Albums had outlived the popularity of the unreliable 8-track tape, and although cassettes would still be around a while longer, they tended to jam, unspool and break. But with compact discs there was finally a commercially available digital audio format and one that was fairly durable as well. According to the article "The Decline of the Compact

Disc" in *Retro Manufacturing*, "By 1985 sales started to grow rapidly. In 1988 CD sales surpassed vinyl LPs, and by 1989 they outsold prerecorded music cassette tapes for the first time ever—thus becoming the most popular audio format." Marion Carter said, "*Beach Beat V* was our last vinyl album with artwork I think, [about] 1987....We did do several hardcore shag tunes LP's with generic covers which came out in the years following, so the last releases of any sort ended somewhere around 1990. I remember that's the year we began stocking CDs, and we issued our first one on Ripete."

Once the industry leader in producing beach music compilation albums ceased pressing LPs, it's not hyperbole to say that, sadly, after less than two decades, beach music compilations on vinyl were basically a thing of the past. While the beach music compilation industry would continue on for a few years after the CD became popular, and vinyl albums such as Warner's *Under the Boardwalk*, Era Record's *Big Beach Sound* and Ripete selections such as *Grand Strand Gold* and others came out, the writing was on the wall. It was the end of the vinyl era and simultaneously the end of the classic years of beach music as well.

WORKS CITED AND OTHER RESOURCES

Abbey, John. "The Whispers Are Getting Louder." http://www.soulmusic.com.

All But Forgotten Oldies. "Interview with Richard Younger. *Get a Shot of Rhythm and Blues: The Arthur Alexander Story.*" www.allbutforgottenoldies.net.

Barker, John. "Summertime's Calling Me." Email to the author. September 26, 2011.

Beachley, Chris. Telephone interviews with the author. October 8 and 12, 2023.

Bell, Archie. "Archie Bell and The Drells." Telephone interview with the author. September 27, 2012.

Benicewitz, Larry. "Remembering Willie Tee." *Blues Art Journal* (November 2007). https://www.bluesart.at.

Bogdanov, Vladimir. *All Music Guide to Soul: The Definitive Guide to R&B and Soul.* Backbeat Books, 2003.

Braheny, John. "Interview with Thom Bell." September 28, 2007. http://johnbraheny.com.

Brewster, Bill, and Frank Broughton. *Last Night a DJ Saved My Life*. Grove Press, 2000.

Bronson, Fred. *The Billboard Book of Number One Hits*. Billboard, 1988.

Broven, John. *Rhythm and Blues in New Orleans*. Pelican Publishing, 1978.

———. *South to Louisiana: The Music of the Cajun Bayous*. Pelican Publishing, 1983.

Bubblegum University. "Black Bubblegum." www.bubblegum-music.com.

Burnett, Norm. "The Tymes." Telephone interview with the author. December 20, 2010.

Butler, Jerry. Telephone interview with the author. October 1, 2012.

Carter, Marion. "Ripete Records." Telephone interview with the author. August 10, 2023.

Cason, Buzz. *The Adventures of Buzz Cason: Living the Rock n' Roll Dream*. Hal Leonard Corp., 2004.

Cermanski, Edward. "The Trammps." E-mails to author. April 15 and 16, 2010.

Channel, Bruce. "Hey! Baby." E-mails to author. August 23, December 19, 2010.

Coasters Web Site. "Those Hoodlum Friends: The Coasters." www.angelfire.com.

Cooper, Francis, and Bill Friskics Warren. "Back With the Beat." *Nashville Scene*. October 12, 1995. http://www.nashvillescene.com.

Curry, Clifford. Telephone interviews with the author. October 31, 2010, February 2, 2011, October 31, 2011.

Dahl, Bill. "Jackie Wilson." Brunswick Records. www.brunswickrecords.com.

————. "Papa Don Schroeder Reminisces about Producing James and Bobby Purify." Sundazed, March 18, 2012. http://www.sundazed.com.

Dawson, Jim, and Steve Propes. *45 RPM: The History, Heroes, and Villains of the Pop Music Revolution.* Backbeat Books, 2003.

————. *What Was the First Rock and Roll Record?* Faber and Faber, 1992.

Deffaa, Chip. *Blue Rhythms: Six Lives in Rhythm and Blues.* Da Capo Press, 1999.

DeYoung, Bill. "Clarence Carter, Soul Man." Connect Savannah. February 9, 2010. http://www.connectsavannah.com.

Dixon, Robert, and John Goodrich. *Blues and Gospel Records, 1890–1943.* Oxford University Press, 1997.

Driggs, Frank, and Chuck Haddix. *Kansas City Jazz: From Ragtime to Bebop—A History.* Oxford University Press, 2006.

Fensterstock, Alison. "Willie Tee." *Gambit,* September 17, 2007. https://www.nola.com/gambit.

Fox, Randy. "Nashville R&B Hero Clifford Curry Dies at 79." *Nashville Scene.* http://www.nashvillescene.com.

Freeland, David. *The Ladies of Soul.* University Press of Mississippi, 2001.

Gardner, Veta, and Earl Gardner. "The Coasters." E-mails to author. July 14 and August 13, 2010.

Gillett, Charlie. "All for One: A Study in Frustration and Black Organization." *Cream,* September 1971. http://www.charliegillett.com.

————. *Making Tracks: Atlantic Records and the Growth of a Billion Dollar Industry.* Dutton, 1974.

Goldberg, Marv. "The Later Drifters." *Marv Goldberg's R&B Notebooks.* https://www.uncamarvy.com.

Grendysa, Peter. "Hello Ruth! The Ruth Brown Story." *It Will Stand* 2, nos. 12, 13 (1980): 4–6.

Hannusch, Jeff. "Obituary: Benny Spellman." *Offbeat Magazine*. https://www.offbeat.com.

Hayes, Bernie. *The Death of Black Radio: The Story of America's Black Radio Personalities.* iUniverse, 2005.

History of Rock. "Jackie Wilson." www.history-of-rock.com.

Houston, Keith. Telephone interview with the author. August 18, 2011.

Jackson, John A. *A House on Fire: The Rise and Fall of Philadelphia Soul.* Oxford University Press, 2004.

James, Gary. Interview with Ben E. King. http://www.classicbands.com.

Jancik, Wayne. *The Billboard Book of One-Hit Wonders.* Billboard Books, 1990.

Kelly, Red. "James and Bobby Purify: So Many Reasons." *The B Side.* http://redkelly.blogspot.com.

Kirby, Michael Jack. "Buster Brown." Way Back Attack. https://www.waybackattack.com.

———. "The Drifters." Way Back Attack. http://www.waybackattack.com.

Kuban, Bob. Telephone interview with the author. August 23, 2010.

Larkin, Colin. *The Encyclopedia of Popular Music.* Oxford University Press, 2000.

Laszewski, Chuck. "'Hello Stranger': Barbara Lewis in Town for 'Taste.'" *MinnPost,* June 30, 2008. https://www.minnpost.com.

Lemon, Meadowlark. "The Globetrotters." Telephone interview with the author. January 11, 2011.

Leszczak, Bob. *The Encyclopedia of Pop Music Aliases, 1950–2000.* Rowman & Littlefield Publishers, 2014.

Lewisohn, Mark. *The Beatles Recording Sessions.* Hyperion, 1992.

Louisiana Music Hall of Fame. "Benny Spellman." louisianamusichalloffame. org.

Lukasavitz, Brian. "Blues Law: Atlantic Records vs. Stax Records." *American Blues Scene*, February 3, 2014. https://www.americanbluesscene.com.

Marsh, Dave. *The Heart of Rock & Soul: The 1001 Greatest Singles Every Made.* Da Capo Press, 1999.

McElrath, John. "Swingin' Medallions." www.medallions.com.

———. Telephone interview with the author. July 19, 2010.

Millar, Bill. "Arthur Alexander." Alabama Music Hall of Fame. www. alamhof.org.

Moore, Bobby, Jr. Telephone interview with the author. November 1, 2010.

Moore, Dave, and Jason Thornton. *The There's That Beat! Guide to The Philly Sound.* Premium Publishing, 2016.

Moore, Deacon John. Telephone interview with the author. November 19, 2010.

Morris, Deane. Telephone interview with the author. 24 July 2013.

Murrells, Joseph. *The Book of Golden Discs: The Records That Sold a Million.* Barrie and Jenkins, 1978.

Musso, Anthony. *Setting the Record Straight.* Author House, 2007.

Newsom, Jim. "Beach Music's Five Star General." General Johnson, American Songwriter. www.generalnormanjohnson.com.

New York Times. "Robert Dickey, 'I'm Your Puppet' Singer, Dies at 72." January 5, 2012.

Owen, James Roberts. "Earl Bostic: Up There in Orbit" 2012. https://digitalcollections.wesleyan.edu/object/ir-1194.

Pareles, John. "Willie Tee, New Orleans Musical Innovator, Dies at 63." *New York Times*, September 13, 2007. https://www.nytimes.com.

Perrone, Pierre. "Bobby Moore: Leader of the Rhythm Aces." *Independent*, March 18, 2006. www.independent.co.uk.

———. "Earl Nelson: Half of Bob and Earl." *Independent.* www.independent.co.uk.

Pittman, Wayne. "The Okaysions." Telephone interview with the author. November 3, 2010.

Pope, Charles. "The Tams." Emails to author. June 25, July 11 and August 23, 25, 27 and 28, 2010.

Pope, Dianne, and Charles Pope. "The Tams." E-mails to author. December 12, 2011, and February 21, 2012.

Pop History Dig. "Hello Stranger." http://www.pophistorydig.com.

Pruter, Robert. *Chicago Soul.* University of Illinois Press, 1991.

Pugh, Fred. Telephone interview with the author. September 11, 2016.

Reid, Jeff. "Blacksmith, Shakers, and etc." E-mail to the author. September 14, 2016.

———. Telephone interview with the author. March 8, 2012.

Retro Manufacturing. "The Decline of the Compact Disc." https://www.retromanufacturing.com.

Roberts, Kev. *The Northern Soul Top 500.* Bee Cool Publishing, 2003.

Rosalsky, Mitch. *Encyclopedia of Rhythm and Blues and Doo Wop Vocal Groups.* Scarecrow Press, 2008.

Sawyer, Phil, and Tom Polland. *Save the Last Dance for Me: A Love Story of the Shag.* University of South Carolina Press, 2012.

Scott, Billy. E-mails to the author. November 10, 2010; July 6 and January 30, 2011; March 3, 7, 8, 9, 10, 11, 2012; September 14, 17, 19, 26, 27 2012; and October 1, 2, 3, 2012.

————. Telephone interviews with the author. November 1, 2010; July 7, 2011.

Selvin, Joel. "Capturing the Beat of the Beach." *San Francisco Examiner,* June 13, 1982.

Shane, Ken. "Soul Serenade: Clarence Carter, 'Slip Away.'" *Popdose,* March 28, 2013.

Smith, Bobbie. "The Spinners." Telephone interview with the author. September 10, 2011.

T5 Pole Position. "The Northern Soul Top 500." https://www.vespa-t5.org.

Tharp, Ammon. "Bill Deal and the Rhondels." Telephone interview with the author. November 10, 2010.

Tims: This is My Story. "Buster Brown." https://tims.blackcat.nl/.

Tomlinson, Bobby. "The Catalinas." Telephone interview with the author. August 1, 2010.

Trexler, Donny. "Bob Collins and the Fabulous Five." Telephone interview with the author. March 9, 2012.

Turner, Sonny. "The Platters." Telephone interview with the author. August 10, 2010.

Wald, Elijah. *How the Beatles Destroyed Rock 'n' Roll: An Alternative History of American Popular Music.* Oxford University Press, 2009.

Warner, Jay. *American Singing Groups*. Hal Leonard Press, 2006.

Washburn, Mark Lawrence Toppmann and April Baker. "Beach Music Icon General Johnson Dies." *Charlotte Observer*, October 17, 2010.

Webb, Robert. "Double Take: 'Hold Back the Night' The Trammps / Graham Parker and the Rumour." *Independent*. www.independent.co.uk.

Weiss, Ed. Telephone interview with the author. August 12, 2010.

Weller, Sheila. *Girls Like Us: Carole King, Joni Mitchell, Carly Simon—and the Journey of a Generation*. Washington Square Press, 2009.

Wells, Robyn. "Beach Beat Records: Surf's Up in Sales." *Billboard*, August 29, 1981.

Whitburn, Joel. *Billboard Hot 100 Charts—The Sixties*. Hal Leonard Corp., 1995.

———. *Bubbling Under the Hot 100, 1959–1985*. Record Research, 1992.

———. *Top Pop Singles, 1955–1986*. Record Research, 1987.

———. *Top R&B Singles, 1942–1995*. Hal Leonard Corp., 1996.

Wicker, Ann. *Making Notes: Music of the Carolinas*. Novello Festival Press, 2008.

Windle, Mark. "Bob Meyer and the Rivieras." *It's Better to Cry*. October 2, 2013. http://southernsoulcollector.blogspot.com.

Younger, Richard. "Arthur Alexander." E-mails to author. October 31 and December 19, 2010.

———. *Get a Shot of Rhythm and Blues: The Arthur Alexander Story*. University of Alabama Press, 2000.

INDEX

Songs

ABOUT THE AUTHOR

*D*r. Rick Simmons was previously the George K. Anding Endowed Professor and Director of Honors at Louisiana Tech University. He is author of more than 130 published works, including 8 books, and his previous works for The History Press include *Carolina Beach Music: The Classic Years* and *Carolina Beach Music from the '60s to the '80s: The New Wave*, as well as *Defending South Carolina's Coast: The Civil War from Georgetown to Little River* and *Hidden History of the Grand Strand*. He currently lives in  Pawleys Island, South Carolina, with his wife, Sue, and teaches at the Georgetown School of Arts and Sciences.

Visit us at
www.historypress.com